CHRÉTIEN AND CANADIAN FEDERALISM

CHRÉTIEN AND CANADIAN FEDERALISM

—⁓—

Politics and the Constitution, 1993–2003

Edward McWhinney

Ronsdale Press

CHRÉTIEN AND CANADIAN FEDERALISM
Copyright © 2003 Edward McWhinney

RONSDALE PRESS
3350 West 21st Avenue
Vancouver, B.C., Canada
V6S 1G7

Typesetting: Julie Cochrane, in New Baskerville 11 pt on 15
Cover Design: Rand Berthaudin, Pause Communications
Paper: Ancient Forest Friendly Rolland "Enviro" — 100% post-consumer waste, totally chlorine-free and acid-free

Ronsdale Press wishes to thank the Canada Council for the Arts, the Government of Canada through the Book Publishing Industry Development Program (BPIDP), and the Province of British Columbia through the British Columbia Arts Council for their support of its publishing program.

National Library of Canada Cataloguing in Publication Data

McWhinney, Edward, 1924–
  Chrétien and Canadian federalism; politics and the constitution, 1993–2003 / Edward McWhinney.

  Includes bibliographical references and index.
  ISBN 1-55380-006-0

  1. Canada — Politics and government — 1993– 2. McWhinney, Edward, 1924–.
  I. Title.
FC635.M39 2003   971.064'8   C2003-910700-0
F1034.2.M39 2003

At Ronsdale Press we are committed to protecting the environment. To this end we are working with Markets Initiative (www.oldgrowthfree.com) and printers to phase out our use of paper produced from ancient forests. This book is one step towards that goal.

Printed in Canada by AGMV Marquis

To the Electors of
Vancouver Quadra

"Your representative owes you, not
his industry only, but his judgement;
and he betrays instead of serving you
if he sacrifices it to your opinion."
— Edmund Burke, *Speech to the Electors of*
Bristol, 3 November 1774.

ACKNOWLEDGEMENTS

The author acknowledges, with thanks, the assistance of Thomas Braun, B.A., LL.B., LL.M., my longtime executive assistant, and of Janice Phillips, my former Ottawa secretary and office manager, for checking and verifying sources in the original McWhinney files from the Centre Block, House of Commons, Ottawa. My thanks also to Anna Trinh, my able Vancouver constituency assistant, for confirming the content of particular case-files, as well as for the contribution she made, together with Ute Gust, in the technical preparation of my manuscript. I am especially grateful to publisher Ronald Hatch for his always helpful advice and criticism. My thanks are also due to editor John Munro for his felicitous guidance in the demanding areas of editorial style and styling, and for the extra counsel he provided on some of the rarer points of Canadian constitutional history. Opinions expressed in the following text are those of the author, unless otherwise expressly acknowledged or cited.

CONTENTS

CHRÉTIEN AND CANADIAN FEDERALISM

INTRODUCTION

Participant Observers and Active Players

My professional life, apart from a few brief years as a trial lawyer and occasional crown prosecutor, has been largely passed in the academies and universities, combined with frequent consulting and advising, internationally and at home (the latter at all three levels — municipal, provincial and federal); and in the service of a number of different political parties. My sometime teacher and later colleague, Harold Lasswell, dean of American social scientists, characterized this sort of combined professional role as that of the *participant-observer.* That is to say that although one is part of the events as they unfold, yet, because of the professional nature of one's engagement in those events, one has to operate within certain accepted scientific standards of commitment to honest identification of the facts, options and costs in a given problem-situation.

There are, in other words, inbuilt obligations of political self-restraint on the part of the participant-observer, and a recognition that the mandate for ultimate political choice and decision must remain with the public officials legitimated by direct election (and with their personal political advisers).

I mention this as prelude to a discussion of some of the experiences provided by the rather rare opportunity opened to me a decade ago when I moved from the ivory towers and the outer ante-rooms of power into the public arenas of political action. It was this special circumstance that now allows me to go beyond the law-in-books — the abstract, *a priori* specifications of institutions and procedures and categories of law-making competences set out in original constitutional charters drafted in an earlier century for a quite different society than our own today — to examine the actual *how, when, why* and *by whom* key community decisions are made. Roscoe Pound, founder of the North American school of sociological jurisprudence, would have called this "law-in-action."

Pound argued that this gap between historical legal prescriptions and the elemental facts-of-life needed to be understood to enable intelligent, purposive programs of change and modernization to be undertaken. Harold Lasswell, who pioneered the field with studies such as *Politics: Who gets What, When, How,* opened up another, too often overlooked element in community decision-making with his 1930 book *Psychopathology and Politics.* It is the personality variable in political leadership which ensures that institutions established either by convention or in constitutional charter may fluctuate wildly in their actual operation as between different incumbents even when of the same political party.

I should state at the outset that this is not a personal biography. The present study is limited in its coverage to the events of the past decade or so in Ottawa, from the early 1990s to the opening of the present century. That is to say, from my first entry into the lists as a candidate for party nomination through my two successive, full terms as an elected Member of Parliament and a member of the government. What I have attempted to do is open some new, realist-inspired perspectives on our constitutional government as it actually operates in our federal system today. I can only hope that the discussions that follow encourage some of my fellow citizens to consider taking their turn as active players in the direct political processes.

The Road to Ottawa

My own entrance to Parliament may well throw some light on the process by which candidates for Parliament are chosen. I had been approached directly in late 1991 by representatives of two major political parties with invitations to meet with their respective leaders to discuss national policies, with a view to my possible candidacy in the forthcoming election. Their interest was not in my then current work in foreign policy and the new, post-détente system of world public order on which I had lectured and commented widely in Canada and abroad in forums as diverse as the Russian Institute of State and Law and the United States House of Representatives Committee on Foreign Affairs. Their emphasis, instead, was on my earlier role as chief adviser (along with distinguished political scientists John Meisel and Léon Dion[1] from Queen's and Laval universities, respectively) to the Trudeau-appointed Pepin-Robarts[2] Task Force on Canadian Unity (1977–1979), from which much of the substance of the Meech Lake Accord, and particularly its provisions on safeguarding the French Language within Quebec, had been borrowed.[3]

---

[1] The father of Stéphane Dion, the minister of intergovernmental affairs in the Chrétien cabinet.

[2] Jean-Luc Pepin, former Trudeau cabinet minister, and John Robarts, former Conservative premier of Ontario.

[3] The Task Force recommended provincial control of language rights; replacing the Senate with a Council of the Federation appointed by the provincial governments; providing the provinces with a "veto" over Supreme Court and certain other important federal appointments; generally reducing federal powers (except with regard to economic management); and introducing limited proportional representation in federal elections.

Initially, however, I was not convinced that I could achieve as much in public, political life as I could in writing, teaching and consulting in my fields of specialization: federalism, constitutionalism, and international law and organization. Then I met with Jean Chrétien in the spring of 1992. The Liberal party leader, whom I already knew, was accompanied by his close adviser, Ross Fitzpatrick, whom I had not met previously.[4] Chrétien asked me to become a candidate. And, after some discussion with family and friends, I accepted his invitation. The timing was right. A number of my longstanding commitments and projects had been completed, providing a rare window of opportunity so far as my private, professional career was concerned.

I was approached shortly after my meeting with Chrétien and Fitzpatrick by Frank Murphy, labour lawyer, Liberal party elder statesman, and the "godfather" of the Vancouver Quadra constituency association which had successfully returned Prime Minister John Turner to Parliament, when his short-lived government (30 June-17 September 1984) was going down to crushing defeat in the rest of the country.[5] Murphy told me that Turner, who in the general elections of 1984 and 1988 was the sole Liberal elected from BC, would not be a candidate for re-election. He also told me that there were a number of candidates already vying for the Quadra nomination, but that the constituency association executive would welcome my candidacy (blessed as it had been by Jean Chrétien). He added, however, that he and the executive would remain neutral and publicly uncommitted in the upcoming nomination contest, as would John Turner (whom I also knew from Montreal and Ottawa).

---

[4] Fitzpatrick would be appointed head of the BC Liberal campaign team in the 1993 general election.

[5] Murphy, his wife Jean and their daughters belonged to that class of enthusiastic and talented amateurs — now, unfortunately, rapidly disappearing from the public political scene — who would give of their time and intellectual energies fully and generously as campaign volunteers, without thought or expectation of material rewards or recognition.

All this meant that there would be no easy, automatic passage to the party's nomination, as would be the case, for example, with a number of leader-sponsored candidates in Quebec and Ontario — and even, in the odd instance, elsewhere. Those favoured few were simply appointed the party's nominees (with constituency association elections dispensed with altogether and other candidates barred). Should I now seek a similar grace-and-favour appointment in Quadra? After discussion with friends who urged such action, I concluded that I should not. On constitutional grounds, such a course would be inconsistent with those basic principles of representative democracy to which I had, over the years, devoted a good part of my teaching, my writing and my life. On purely political grounds, it would be quite unfair to the other candidates, who had entered the field in good faith and in expectation of a fair and open contest. My *modus operandi* was clear: (1) to enter the existing nomination battle; (2) to make up lost ground by a vigorous campaign focusing on key policy issues; and (3) to win. This we did, eleven months later in March 1993, in a come-from-behind victory, lasting through four ballots and a full seven hours until one o'clock in the morning. It was an exhilarating, if exhausting experience. The deliberate concentration on issues — a battle of ideas — normally lacking in party nomination contests, brought us our core organization.[6]

In agreeing to seek the Liberal nomination in the summer of 1992 (before the Charlottetown referendum), it was in clear expectation of what I might offer the party by way of constitutional expertise, if and when that party should form a government. It was not until well into the 1993 election campaign itself that it became

---

[6] My nomination campaign team — median age twenty-three — was directed by a triumvirate from the University of British Columbia: Mark Cameron, Thomas Braun and Eric Lay. A small "ginger" group of young volunteers, including Jim Paloubis, Kirsten Jensen, Tony Fogarassy, Blair Lockhart and Chris Gignac, helped develop nomination tactics. Advice on overall strategy came from experienced volunteers, such as Betty Trainor and Stephen Sander. We also had a wise, experienced teacher and former member of the Vancouver School Board, Harkirpal Singh Sara (the first

apparent that the constitution and Quebec were no longer important to voters, or even issues that they wanted to discuss at all. The
key issue for the Canadian voter had become the economy. In the
words of the electoral slogan that the United States Democratic
party so successfully used against incumbent President George
H.W. Bush (the Gulf War victor in 1990–1991) in defeating his re-
election bid in November 1992: "It's the economy, stupid!"

Mulroney to Chrétien

An understanding of the Chrétien decade from 1993 to 2003 must
necessarily be built on the principles and practices of the immediate past. The Conservative government elected under Prime Minister Brian Mulroney in mid-1984 had proceeded triumphantly
with an agenda of change — *triadic* change of a revolutionary character as it turned out, in terms of long-range consequences for
Canadian federalism and Canadian society as a whole. The first
element in the Mulroney program was borrowed directly from one
of those interminable and expensive royal commissions of enquiry
spawned by its predecessor Liberal government. The Macdonald
Commission, chaired by a former Trudeau cabinet minister, had
recommended in its 1985 multi-volume report that Canada enter
into a bilateral, free-trade agreement with the United States. Mulroney saw an opportunity in this for a political breakthrough and,
in words Disraeli had used a century earlier, caught the Liberals
bathing and ran away with their clothes. Free trade had been a
plank in Laurier's unsuccessful campaign for re-election in 1911. A
Conservative government three quarters of a century later seized
the idea and successfully negotiated it with the United States. In

---

Sikh-Canadian to hold elected municipal office in Vancouver), as chair of
our cultural and policy committee. In 1993, my election campaign was run
by Thomas Braun, Elizabeth Murphy and Jim Paloubis (with Craig Munroe
as university student liaison and Peter Szeto as the candidate's aide), supported by an army of volunteers from all the main riding communities. The
Quadra constituency association executive, under president Bob Carveth,
played a key role throughout both the 1993 and 1997 general election campaigns.

another historical irony, the Liberal party, under Trudeau's successor as leader, John Turner, fought the 1988 election in opposition to the free-trade agreement, with the promise that, if elected, he would tear up the agreement and insist on renegotiating its terms. Turner lost that election, and the Canada-United States Agreement, as already signed, sealed and delivered legally, was politically vindicated.

This was soon followed by a trilateral Canada-USA-Mexico free-trade treaty, based on the general model of the Canada-United States bilateral agreement, and again successfully negotiated by Mulroney. The North American Free Trade Agreement (NAFTA) held forth the political promise of possible further openings to other states in Central and South America, if and when they should attain comparable levels in their financial and general economic systems to those of the three original signatories. Continentalism — in the sense of transnational cooperation and coordination of trade and commerce, and possible eventual integration on a hemispherical basis — was thus opened up. Its long-range consequences, political as well as economic, may have been envisaged by the political leaders at the time, but these certainly were not generally comprehended or considered by the Canadian voting public.

A third element in the Mulroney agenda of fundamental change for Canada had to do with the constitution, and with achieving what largely had eluded both Prime Ministers Pearson and Trudeau: coming to grips with the challenge of Quebec's "quiet revolution." This meant, first, ascertaining, in the trite political phrase of the times: "What does Quebec want?" Conclusions then had to be refined and rationalized on a basis that would be politically acceptable to the rest of Canada, and thus capable of being adopted as a formal amendment to the constitution of Canada under the formula embodied in the Constitution Act of 1982.[7]

---

[7] Under section 42 (1)(c) of the Constitution Act of 1982, this can only be effected by the difficult constitutional amending processes established under Article 38(1) of the same Act — namely, by Senate and House resolutions, accompanied by similar resolutions of the legislatures of at least two-thirds of the provinces, including either Quebec or Ontario.

Here, however, Mulroney encountered failure. It was a near-miss, as much the result of overconfidence on Mulroney's part as it was the product of any unwillingness in English-speaking Canada — or, more particularly, of the provincial premiers directly involved in the negotiations for a constitutional amendment — to make a generous response to the rejection of sovereignty- association by Quebec voters in the 1980 referendum. This was the spectacular failure of Meech Lake: the popular code name of a federal-provincial heads-of-government agreement, adopted unanimously in 1987, which provided for a substantial decentralization of the federal system, as well as a recognition of Quebec's claims to a constitutional "particularity" through a legally protected status for the French language and culture within Quebec itself. It was this agreement that induced Quebec's then Liberal premier, Robert Bourassa, to express his faith in the Canadian federal system. Indeed, all the provincial premiers put their signatures to the document, and pledged to ratify Meech Lake by vote of their respective legislatures — the procedure legally necessary and sufficient, with a similar vote by the federal Parliament to adopt the agreement's proposals as part of the Constitution of Canada. This, however, was not to be.

Prime Minister Mulroney, surprisingly, had allowed too long a time-frame for the necessary resolutions of the provincial legislatures. As the three-year deadline approached in 1990, significant changes among the heads of provincial governments occurred. The long-serving Conservative premier of New Brunswick, Richard Hatfield, was defeated and replaced by Meech Lake skeptic, Liberal Frank McKenna, who simply sat on his hands and took no action. A friendly NDP (New Democratic party) premier of Manitoba, Howard Pawley, also departed after an electoral defeat. Newfoundland experienced a similar sea-change. And, as if this were not difficulty enough, the three-year delay between negotiation and signature of the Meech Lake intergovernmental accord and its constitutional ratification encouraged assorted political pressure groups that had been silent or unorganized in the rush of events in 1987 to lobby at the provincial level in attempts to block ratification. In particular, aboriginal leaders and their organizations, not having been invited and therefore not present at the creation as new "founding fathers" in 1987, mounted a very effective campaign, especially in the key holdout province of Manitoba.

When Meech Lake failed, Mulroney attempted a new constitutional initiative, the Charlottetown Agreement. This was different, in structure and design, as well as in phrasing and style to the Meech Lake Accord, perhaps in considerable measure because of the departure from the prime minister's office of Norman Spector, who, in large part, had guided the Meech Lake process. Meech Lake had represented the quest for a new equilibrium of federal institutions, and in the political forces operating through them. It had not hesitated to embrace new concepts — "asymmetrical federalism" was a prime example — designed to recognize and accommodate regional particularisms in constitutional form. It was, for this reason, something that required a considerable amount of explanation and education in its defence as the public debate mounted during the three-year interval between adoption of the original agreement and the final cutoff for ratification as a constitutional amendment.

The Charlottetown Agreement, in contrast, was more down-to-earth. Its substance was easier to comprehend, without too much need for technical legal interpretation. But this also meant that the incidental political horse-trading necessary to secure its preliminary adoption — again by a heads-of-government consensus — was exposed much more clearly to public view, and consequent criticism. Mulroney, to counter charges of *elitism* leveled against the essentially oligarchic, intergovernmental process that had been followed throughout the Meech Lake exercise, made a symbolic gesture to Trudeau-style participatory democracy. In a "gambler's throw," he submitted the Charlottetown Agreement to a nation-wide referendum. Public support thus enlisted, he believed, would compel a prompt across-the-board ratification of the Agreement by the provincial legislatures as a constitutional amendment. This was a bold move. It reflected Mulroney's confidence in direct democracy and its impact on political decision-makers. Certainly, his position contrasted sharply with the arcane process and behind-the-scenes negotiation and bargaining effectively enjoined by the new constitutional amending machinery established under the Trudeau government's Constitution Act of 1982.

From the outset, however, the Charlottetown Agreement's acceptance appeared to be imperilled by a provision guaranteeing Quebec one-quarter of all the seats in the House of Commons, for all time and irrespective of any future changes in Quebec's percentage of the total population of Canada (predicted by most demographers as certain to continue to decline). There had been enough criticisms of the marked imbalance in Quebec's existing representation in the non-elected Senate — twenty-four seats in comparison to the same number for the whole of Western Canada (six for BC and for each of the three prairie provinces) — to ensure a hostile reaction. The well-meaning premier of British Columbia, Mike Harcourt, as a gesture of generosity and goodwill, had accepted the proposed fixed quota for Quebec of twenty-five percent of the Commons seats on the promise of some extra seats for BC. But this was not nearly enough to placate the fierce opposition which began on Vancouver's open-line radio shows, then swept like a tidal wave across the country. Charlottetown was lost, irretrievably, in every province but Ontario, which approved it, marginally, in the popular vote. Even Quebec voters said NO (with some considerable encouragement from Pierre Trudeau).[8]

With the failure of the Charlottetown Agreement, the great debate that had raged for three decades over "What does Quebec want?" and "What are Quebec's proper constitutional powers and role in the Canadian federal system?" came to an end. What was not apparent at the time was whether this would be a temporary respite, or a long-term situation. The Mulroney government, in its

---

[8] My own, soon-to-be constituency of Vancouver Quadra was a rare BC exception, where voters said YES.

effort to bring this critical debate to a successful conclusion with constitutional changes that could be justified in Quebec as meeting its "quiet revolution" imperatives, had prolonged its second term in office, deliberately, from the customary four years to the full statutory limit of five years, thus delaying the general election until October 1993. Its options as to the timing of the election, and thus of having some margin of choice in determining the key policy issues to bring to the voters, had simply run out.

The failure of Meech Lake, and the subsequent delays in preparing Charlottetown, followed by its failure, destroyed a planned orderly transition of power within the ruling Conservative party. Indeed, a brokered succession to a new leader, who — on the happy precedents of the Ontario Conservative party which had retained power for more than four decades by changing its leader every decade — ideally would be seen by the electorate as embodying new thinking and innovative approaches to contemporary problems. In the result, however, everything had to be arranged in an unseemly rush, without enough time for any new party leader to establish a positive personality imprint in the public mind, or to mount a distinctive campaign, with sufficient distance from the departing chief.

The most obvious comparison was that of John Turner in July 1984, trying in the two months available to him as the new Liberal party leader, to disengage himself from the political baggage accumulated during Pierre Trudeau's sixteen years in power. Kim Campbell, in 1993, had a scant four months to escape the general public backlash and political odium now attaching to the two successive failed constitution-making exercises of Meech Lake and Charlottetown. The electoral outcome was a complete disaster for Campbell and the Conservatives. The once proud party of Sir John A. Macdonald was reduced to two seats in the House of Commons, and Canada's first woman prime minister went down to bitter personal defeat in her own constituency of Vancouver Centre.

Jean Chrétien, on the other hand, had appeared to emerge from the constitutional debacle blameless in the public mind. He had opposed Meech Lake, but, paradoxically perhaps, had then supported Charlottetown and had taken part in the YES campaign — by which time he was leader of the opposition and preparing for the general election the following year. Undoubtedly, he was aware that his anti-Meech Lake position had cost him critical support among francophone Quebecers whose votes could be pivotal in producing in what was then considered to be a best case scenario: a minority government. Certainly, the focus of the Liberal party at the time, in terms of candidate selection and campaign issues, was, as with other national parties, still on the constitution and Quebec.

In my own chosen constituency, Vancouver Quadra, the electors from all cultural communities expressed a deep concern about the huge annual budgetary deficit — $42.8 billion in the last budget brought in by the Mulroney government — and a fear of an economic recession combining the twin evils of high unemployment and high inflation. The message eventually filtered through to the upper strata of command in the rival political parties. Although the practice of annual deficit budgets at the federal level had been introduced more than two decades earlier under Trudeau, the incumbent Conservative government bore the brunt of the responsibility, public blame, and consequent electoral censure.

Canadians elected a Liberal majority government in October 1993, albeit one with a very small majority. The Conservatives, as noted above, were decimated. Reduced to two MPs, they lost official party status. The *Bloc Québécois* separatist party became the official opposition. The balance of those opposite was split between the Western-based, conservative Reform party and the painfully reduced, social democratic NDP. Significantly, in a House of two hundred and ninety-five members, two hundred and eight had been elected for the first time.

The new Liberal majority was heavily concentrated in the province of Ontario, where it had almost swept the board, with a hundred members — almost two-thirds of our total in the House. This made for a potentially unhealthy imbalance within the government majority and, ultimately, within the federal system as a whole.

Political power was seen to be effectively concentrated in the wealthiest and most heavily industrialized of Canada's provinces. It invited historical comparisons with other federal systems, most notably Germany under the Bismarckian constitution of 1871 and that of the ill-fated Weimar Republic of 1919, where the same extreme disproportions in electoral weight and influence of the core component, Prussia, had contributed to and hastened the ultimate decline of the whole state. With a representation from British Columbia of only six members out of a total of thirty-two for the province, BC's Liberal MPs were outnumbered more than sixteen times to one by those from Ontario (and even seven times to one by the metropolitan Toronto regional sub-caucus within the larger Ontario delegation).[9] Consequently, cabinet building by the new prime minister would require some special care and concern, particularly in view of the startling numerical weakness in Liberal representation in Western Canada.

In some degree, the 1993 election also may have turned, in the end, on *non-policy* issues such as the voters' desire for *change* from the high-pitched excitement of the Mulroney years (and those of Trudeau), with their emphasis on high deficit spending and on apparently interminable, wholly non-productive constitutional debates and quarrels at the expense of serious and sober discussion of financial and economic issues (notably individual employment and well-being). The Liberal return to power was also affected, strongly, and unexpectedly favourably, by the casual elements of personality and leadership style. The Conservative party's campaign had focused on change, fundamental change, as represented by Kim Campbell, their new young female leader and prime minister, purportedly able to chart a new course without too many backward glances at the retiring Brian Mulroney. The Conservative strategists deliberately characterized Jean Chrétien as "yesterday's man" — a phase lifted out the Liberal party's own 1989 leadership contest between Chrétien and Paul Martin, Jr. The

---

[9] Not counting Senators.

implication, then as now, was that Chrétien had no new ideas and no serious interest in or energy for policy issues.

The Liberal party public relations team countered this with a strategy of emphasizing their leader's age and long practical experience within government in contrast to the new Conservative leader's relatively sparse record and her admitted absence of skills in fiscal management — the key, genuine policy issue emerging in the course of the general election campaign. In the happy formulation by our campaign strategists: "When the ship of state is in stormy waters, you turn to the older steersman to bring it safely into port." A politically unfortunate blunder by the Conservative brains trust in the last two weeks of the campaign in an advertisement focusing on Chrétien's childhood-illness-induced facial tic turned a then impending Conservative government defeat into a rout.[10]

Against this background, the 208 *new* MPs elected to a House of Commons totalling 295 members — an unprecedented percentage of turnover — came to Ottawa with enthusiasm and high hopes of making their influence felt. They would soon come up against the constitutional-governmental reality — the law-in-action as opposed to the ideal, law-in-books as originally written in the constitutional charter of 1867. The system had experienced no fundamental, comprehensive revision and up-dating or even review of its key decision-making institutions and processes over the intervening century and a quarter; although it was now being called on to resolve and harmonize the competing social, cultural and economic interests and demands of a new plural, multi-cultural society totally different from that of 1867. In noting the widening gap between contemporary community demands and expectations and the ability of the system to deliver, one would sometimes be tempted to make comparisons to the arcane processes of decision of the Byzantine Empire in its declining years.

---

[10] In my riding of Vancouver Quadra, we were able to augment John Turner's winning plurality by some sixty percent, and to achieve the largest margin of victory by any Liberal in the province.

I

—∿—

"PRESIDENTIAL"
PRIME-MINISTERSHIP

The emergence of a "presidential" (sometimes called "imperial")
prime-ministership is a phenomenon not limited to Canada or to
other constitutional systems that have evolved, historically, from
the Westminster model. It is a main consequence of the overall
decline of Parliament and of legislative arenas generally, and of
the concentration of effective decision-making power in the executive. The increasing complexity and detail of contemporary problems limit the practical ability of elected parliamentarians, who
must constantly prepare for re-election, to handle and resolve the
intricate problems of governing today. French constitutionalists,
commenting on the constitution of the Fifth Republic (created in
the image and reflecting the personality of wartime Free French
leader, General Charles de Gaulle), were the first to speak of an
"imperial presidency."

The Fifth Republic had been necessitated by the political collapse of the postwar (1946–1958) Fourth Republic, which had seen a rapid succession of weak coalition governments that were widely, if unfairly, blamed for the French military disasters in Vietnam and Algeria. The Fifth Republic, in reaction to the perceived faults of the Fourth Republic, embraced the constitutional corrective of a preponderant executive, concentrated in the office of the president. The presidency would very soon be augmented further, in its political legitimacy, by constitutional amendment giving it the plebiscitarian authority of direct, nationwide popular election. The prefix "imperial" seems then to have been ascribed by academic commentators less as a recognition of the constitutional fact of the location of effective power under the Fifth Republic than as a taking note of the immense popularity of the new office of president under an unbroken succession of very interesting and dynamic leaders: de Gaulle, Pompidou, Giscard d'Estaing and Mitterand.

The office of prime minister emerged in Britain from the early eighteenth century onwards through constitutional custom and convention — practice accepted as sensible and reasonable in relation to the main political players, and legally concretized as such over the ensuing years. At the time of the enactment of Canada's Constitution Act (British North America Act) of 1867, it was not considered necessary to include any definition of the colonial version of this office, or its mandate and powers. It is, in fact, not mentioned in the Act of 1867 or in any of the successive amendments to that Act, including the most recent Constitution Act of 1982. In post-1867 history within the Canadian constitutional system, the "received" British office of prime minister tended to mirror developments in Britain itself, with no tendency within Canada to develop independent initiatives in response to conceived special Canadian conditions.

In Britain, the office, since remaining undefined in constitutional or statutory terms, has been able to change very easily, usually in measure of the personality of the incumbent of the day. For example, two world wars saw an enormous concentration of power in the executive head: in World War I after the politically driven Lloyd George had succeeded the more measured and consensus-oriented Asquith; and in World War II after Neville Chamberlain had been replaced by Winston Churchill. Neither Lloyd George nor Churchill was to survive very long after hostilities ended and peace was restored.[11]

The more dramatic expansion of the role and effective power of the prime minister seems to have come in peacetime, but not merely because of the incremental changes in executive-legislative institutional relations and of what has been called the "Passing of Parliament," with the proliferation of administrative, executive-decree-based law.[12] It is also attributable to the remarkable person-alization of power with the new "hot" forms of communication and the charismatic political leaders who have emerged in the televi-sion era of political campaigning. The office of prime minister in Britain clearly acquired a constitutional amplitude under Margaret Thatcher that it did not have under her predecessor, James Calla-ghan, or her own immediate successor, John Major.

In Canada, the television age would later produce the strong, charismatic leaders, Trudeau and then Mulroney, who would give the Canadian prime-ministership its contemporary "presidential" stamp. The consequence, with clear majority government, was the prime minister's dominance not only over Parliament, but also over cabinet and the government party itself. Policy-formation and also policy application in its larger form became concentrated in the prime minister's office and in the cadre of personal advisers appointed by the prime minister himself and directly responsible and answerable to the prime minister alone.

---

[11] Lloyd George's all-party wartime coalition broke up soon after hostilities ceased, and he was forced into the political wilderness for the remainder of his career. Churchill was voted out by the British electorate in the brief span between the German and Japanese surrenders in 1945, though he did return briefly, in visibly declining health, in 1951, after the attrition of the Attlee Labour government.

[12] See further explanation on p. 137.

Prime Minister's Office — "The Kitchen Cabinet"

Recent media focus has been directed most intensely to the prime minister's office under Jean Chrétien. He, however, has done no more than follow trends already well established under Trudeau and Mulroney — trends he had ample opportunity to study as a member of successive Trudeau cabinets and then as leader of the opposition during the last years of the Mulroney era. A series of uniformly bright, well-educated, young and ambitious people passed through the prime minister's office (PMO) and the related privy council office (PCO[13]) during Trudeau's decade and a half as prime minister. Some examples are Marc Lalonde (before being elected to the House and elevated to ministerial rank); Gordon Gibson (briefly, before becoming disillusioned with Trudeau and returning to Vancouver); Michael Pitfield and Michael Kirby (both later passing to the Senate); Jim Coutts[14] (who would go on to run unsuccessfully, twice, for the House of Commons in the attempt to move, like Marc Lalonde, from the role of private adviser on policy to one of its public executors); Colin Kenny (also to the Senate); and not least, Joyce Fairbairn, who guarded the inner office and had last word on what communications Prime Minister Trudeau would see and on who would get through the front door (she also went on to the Senate). This personal adviser function requires fine judgment since it involves a large discretion which must be exercised with both tact and authority.

Mulroney, of course, brought his own team into the PMO and PCO. I had dealings, in particular, with Norman Spector, a deputy

---

[13] For a discussion of the development of the Privy Council Office since its inception in 1940, see Donald J. Savoie's *Governing from the Centre: The Concentration of Power in Canadian Politics*. Toronto: University of Toronto Press, 1999.

[14] I had some professional dealings with Jim Coutts in the run-up to Prime Minister Trudeau's constitutional "patriation" project which became, eventually, the Constitution Act of 1982. Coutts was quick to comprehend constitutional minutiae and to put them into a larger policy perspective, but he was not brought early enough into the patriation-project team, which may explain why the project's later political difficulties could not all be corrected in time.

minister in British Columbia under the Social Credit administration of Premier Bill Bennett. When Bennett stepped down in 1986, Spector moved to Ottawa. Norman Spector had a doctorate in political psychology (an uncommon credential for a politicologue) and excellent powers of analysis. He also possessed that rare ability for a personal political adviser to relate abstract, ideal-constructs to day-by-day political reality — in short, common-sense appreciation of the art and also the limits of the politically possible. When Spector joined the Mulroney staff, I had discussions with him about the passage of the Meech Lake Accord and its adoption as a formal constitutional amendment. It was he who telephoned me in China, where I was lecturing at the University of Beijing, to return immediately to Canada to testify before a parliamentary committee.[15]

Jean Chrétien, as prime minister, operated at two levels in terms of personal political advisers — through the prime minister's office, but also with a more informal, unsalaried group along the lines of the "kitchen cabinet" made famous by President Franklin Roosevelt, and continued by some of his successors. BC's most important kitchen cabinet member was Ross Fitzpatrick (Senator Fitzpatrick, as he is now). He and Chrétien had become fast friends in the early 1960s during Mike Pearson's first minority government, when Fitzpatrick was executive assistant to Jack Nicholson, one of the two ministers from BC. Fitzpatrick was later to be active in both Chrétien leadership bids. And during Chrétien's absence from politics in the mid to late 1980s, he used his experience as a mining and financial consultant to help Chrétien build up his personal investment portfolio. I came to appreciate Fitzpatrick's keen sense of electoral tactics during the 1993 campaign in BC, which he

---

[15] I approached Prime Minister Mulroney through Spector in late 1990 to ask the prime minister to throw his support behind Egyptian deputy prime minister and minister of state for foreign affairs, Boutros Boutros-Ghali, in his bid to become secretary-general of the United Nations. Still later, in 1995, when Boutros-Ghali was a candidate for re-election as secretary-general, Prime Minister Chrétien agreed to intervene personally to accord him Canada's full support. Unfortunately, his re-election bid failed when vetoed by the United States in the UN security council.

directed. From the single BC seat held by John Turner in Vancouver Quadra, Fitzpatrick made the right tactical choices in the expenditure of political capital to increase this to six Liberal victories in that year's election. With others in charge for the next two elections, our vote plummeted. In the 2000 election, we only won five seats out of a possible thirty-four.

I personally assumed two major policy assignments during the first two years following my election in 1993. First, I endeavoured to make the case for investment by the national government in pure research in advanced science and medicine and technology; and, in particular, the case for the allocation of $167.5 million from the then extreme austerity federal budgets to the TRIUMF advanced physics project at the University of British Columbia (UBC). Second, I argued for government assistance to keep alive Canadian Airlines with its 17,000 highly skilled employees in Western Canada. I called on Fitzpatrick for help from his then post in private life outside the direct political sphere. His political support was crucial in the ultimate success on both fronts, though this was to be a temporary respite only for Canadian Airlines.

In his personal *modus operandi*, Fitzpatrick was polite and soft-spoken, but always in full command of the facts. When a BC vacancy occurred in the Senate in 1997, I felt (and said so) that Fitzpatrick would be a politically sensible and also generally acceptable choice. He was someone who held the personal confidence of the prime minister, who so often turned to him for advice. Consequently, it would be constitutionally more appropriate to render Fitzpatrick's role public, even if this should mean some reduction in his effective range of influence, which I think in fact turned out to be the case.

The Chrétien "kitchen cabinet" also included the prime minister's first mentor in Ottawa. This was Mitchell Sharp, to whom Chrétien became parliamentary secretary in 1966.[16] Sharp later sponsored Chrétien, who was then only thirty-three years old, for

---

[16] Jean Chrétien, who was first elected to the House of Commons in 1963, was briefly parliamentary secretary to Prime Minister Pearson in 1965.

his first cabinet post in 1967 (and for other posts thereafter, including Indian affairs and northern resources in 1968). Sharp, who was an economist by training and a former civil servant, was seen as belonging to the conservative wings of the Pearson and Trudeau administrations. His influence on Chrétien, as prime minister, was generally considered to have been at its peak during the transition days in late 1993, when the new administration was being formed.

As an older Liberal, Sharp tended to focus on those who had already served in Parliament or had worked for the party organization, rather than on any newcomers. This may have accounted, in part, for the seemingly rather conservative, stand-pat cast of the first Chrétien cabinet — no really startling or very interesting breakthroughs in terms of new people or fresh ideas. On some issues of government restructuring and the possible creation of new portfolios or new sub-ministries, Sharp, with his wealth of experience in government, would have been in a position to give decisive advice. However, the few changes that Chrétien actually made seem to have built on innovations, as to nomenclature at least, already ventured upon by the short-lived Kim Campbell Conservative government.

Within the formal group of salaried political advisers in the PMO, the two who stood out and were certainly most identified in the public mind were Jean Pelletier and Eddie Goldenberg. As the people closest to the prime minister, they were consciously silent and reclusive as to any public role. This was something that may have required considerable self-discipline for Jean Pelletier in view of his past considerable success as a municipal politician. I had met him at the opening of the 1980s, when I was constitutional adviser to the Federation of Canadian Municipalities (FCM) during the Trudeau constitutional "patriation" round. Pelletier was, at the time, a high profile and well-regarded Mayor of Quebec City.[17]

---

[17] The FCM's task force on the constitution had put forward an innovative set of proposals for a new, "third level" of government status for municipalities and regional councils in any new or renewed Canadian federal system. This involved participation, with a fixed, municipal quota, in existing federal-

He would also twice be a candidate, unsuccessfully, for election to the Parliament from Quebec City under the Liberal banner.

As an experienced politician, Pelletier seemed a little more combative in his approach than Goldenberg. No doubt for this reason, he tended to be viewed by caucus more as an "enforcer" — the senior partner in a law firm who traditionally says NO and metes out punishment. I think this judgment was unwarranted. Pelletier never, in my observation, went beyond his instructions from above. I had only one minor disagreement with him. This involved an apparent "turf war" with a neighbouring Liberal MP who had complained to him about my alleged interference in that colleague's constituency affairs.

On arriving one afternoon at the airport in Vancouver from the United Nations in New York, I was asked by a local senior legal counsel if I would intervene in a deportation case. The request was made on very convincing humanitarian grounds. The first, urgent step was to rescue an immigrant family with two young children from a plane due to leave in two hours for the former Soviet Union. With no time to ascertain the constituency in which this family might be resident, I responded at once. Immigration Canada kindly granted a temporary stay (the minister, Lucienne Robillard, much later would approve a permanent visa). I explained these facts to Pelletier, to his apparent satisfaction, and indicated that I would be happy to have all credit for this successful operation go to my disgruntled colleague. I was, however, surprised at the intervention by the PMO in a matter so easily and amicably resolved at

---

provincial tax-sharing agreements, and also a municipal law-making competence as to certain local questions constitutionally reserved for the provinces. Prime Minister Trudeau, who was at the time battling against the "gang of eight" group of provincial premiers, was in search of potential allies in the constitutional war. He indicated interest in studying the FCM task force's report. Indeed, the report itself and its recommendations for constitutional change seemed headed for full endorsement at the FCM annual meeting. Then, under apparent political pressures from Premier Lévesque and his *Parti Québécois* government of Quebec, the Quebec municipal delegation withdrew their support for the report, which thereupon was shelved.

lower levels of political responsibility without any need for a ukase from above.

Eddie Goldenberg was unknown to me until the election of 1993, when he accompanied Chrétien on his BC campaign swings. But I had, from my Montreal days, known his father, Senator Carl Goldenberg, a well-known labour lawyer and labour arbitrator, who had been briefly a constitutional adviser to Prime Minister Trudeau during the late 1960s or early 1970s.[18] I found the son a rather shy man, absorbed in his work at the PMO, which seemed preemptive of everything else. But he always responded promptly when called, and could be guaranteed to study, in depth, any documents sent to him. His responses were always helpful. Whenever I had anything of major importance to raise with the prime minister, I usually first communicated with Goldenberg. I made a point, however, of only approaching the PMO in exceptional cases. That said, my communications extended not merely to technical issues, constitutional and other, but to high political developments, including discretionary federal prerogative appointments, both for BC and nationally.

Cabinet — "Supporting Players"

The classical conception of the cabinet has it functioning as a collegial institution, with the prime minister presiding very much like a university faculty dean, with a free exchange of opinion and discussion around the cabinet table, and with decision by emerging collective consensus without any need for formal recorded division or vote. This was no doubt a reasonably correct description of British constitutional practice in the nineteenth and early twentieth centuries. Prime Minister Herbert Asquith, from 1908 on, had presided in very much this way over a Liberal ministry of exceptional

---

[18] Carl Goldenberg's style was Pearson-like in its approach to federal-provincial relations. The Pearson preference was for "cooperative federalism," with an emphasis on pragmatic give-and-take and patient negotiation in conflict-resolution, rather than on declarations of political war.

talents that had included Sir Edward Grey, R.B. Haldane, Lloyd George and the young Winston Churchill. Asquith's government was finally displaced in 1916 at the height of World War I by an all-party wartime coalition, headed by Lloyd George and without Asquith himself. Cabinets were, at the time, very much smaller, and the distinction between the *inner* cabinet and *outer* cabinet was much more marked. World War I and World War II each saw, very quickly, the introduction of coalition governments with inner cabinets of no more than a handful of senior ministers, often freed altogether from departmental charges so that they could give all their time and energies to macro-policy issues.

Within Canada, cabinets have grown larger and larger, no doubt because of the felt necessity in forming any Canadian ministry in modern times to conciliate and provide symbolic representation for as many different and diverse regional, religious, ethnocultural, and other interests as possible — including, even more so today, gender interests. It is also a way of keeping rank-and-file MPs in a government party happy. Large cabinets significantly increase the chances of their eventually making the jump to a ministerial or sub-ministerial post of some form. The fact remains that the full cabinet in Canada is actually larger than the cabinet in the United States, and very much larger, in relation to the total population, than similar bodies in Britain and other western or western-influenced constitutional systems.

Among the national cabinets of the postwar period, the Pearson government (1963–1968) and the short-lived Joe Clark government (1979–1980) seem to have been closest to the classical paradigm of collegial, consensus decision-making bodies. Contrary to much that has been written of late, Trudeau, throughout his long term as prime minister, was mainly interested in constitutional issues, with some attention to foreign policy during his last years in office. In practice, he left a very great autonomy of operation to those of his ministers charged with financial and business portfolios and the larger macro-economic policies that went with them. The same might be said of Mulroney with his preemptive concerns with federal and Quebec issues, foreign policy, international trade, and relations with the United States. That gave a large margin of operation for ministers charged with the more technical, domestic portfolios.

Chrétien had pledged, while leader of the opposition, to cut down on wasteful public expenditures, and to trim the size of government itself. In terms of actual numbers of full ministers, he delivered on that electoral promise, but he added some new, ancillary government posts identified as secretaries of state. These did not carry full ministerial status and their incumbents were not permitted to speak or intervene at cabinet meetings except when expressly invited to do so. This was a twilight, limbo category of governmental post, with the numbers augmented still further by retention, in numerical depth, of that other junior-level appointment inherited from British constitutional practice, the parliamentary secretary.

In Britain, and to some extent with earlier Canadian administrations, these lower-level, supporting posts had been consciously employed as training grounds for promising new players, with a view to testing their capacities for promotion, long range, to senior portfolios. Almost without exception in the successive Chrétien administrations, no such promotions occurred. When the few cabinet changes that did occur took place, it was often done with MPs freshly plucked from the ranks without any prior governmental experience. With the parliamentary secretaries, the practice was to retain them for two years, then return them to their former backbench assignments. This was something that, understandably, produced disaffection within the ranks for those who felt that they had an opportunity for advancement and had performed well, only to have their hopes dashed. In certain cases they may have believed that they had performed at least as well, or better than the ministers they were designated to support. What is more, there were a number of other MPs within caucus who agreed, more or less openly, with that assessment.

Prime Minister Chrétien prided himself on having very little or no turnover within cabinet, and more than once he noted aloud that he had, unlike some earlier administrations, not had to lose a minister because of personal scandals or other misdemeanors. That was true enough in the period 1993–2000, but the price to be paid was a consequent lack of opportunity for the prime minister to make creative choices of new personnel. As the years passed, there was within the government a rather static condition as to policy-formation, and an absence of innovation or of fresh ideas generally. This situation was not so obvious within either the Trudeau or Mulroney administrations.

Certainly, Chrétien always placed a premium on feeling comfortable with his ministerial team. This too often guided his choices for promotion to those who had worked for him in his leadership campaigns. The exclusion of those who had worked for other leadership candidates could hardly be overlooked, particularly in Ontario where, after the 1993 and 1997 general elections, the Liberals held all but one or two of that province's hundred-plus seats. The prime minister would remark in caucus, in the presence of his ministers, that he could form a second or third team, chosen from party ranks in the House, of equal calibre and weight to his first team. This was more widely accepted than perhaps it was intended to be, and it added to the frustrations of those backbenchers who felt they had been unfairly passed over. Even if offered in jest, it had a dangerous element of prophesy in it.

Drawing so fully on those he knew and trusted, the prime minister had a cadre with parliamentary and some prior governmental experience. However, for those who came directly into the cabinet or supporting government posts after the 1993 election without any previous relevant experience, their first appointments probably were mixed blessings at best. These newcomers, often having been chosen (or so it seemed) only to satisfy deemed regional or ethnocultural or other discrete and insular considerations, never really had time to master the basic skills involved in being Members of Parliament. A number of them were to go down to electoral defeat in 1997, even in supposedly safe party seats.

And some of the job descriptions for the newer cabinet or para-cabinet posts might make even angels fear to tread, the parameters of relevance being ill-defined or open-ended at best. Did the person in the PMO who first dreamed up the new post of secretary of state (Asia-Pacific) have even elementary comprehension of the inherited historical ruptures within the vast Asian continent, or the intrinsic cultural, linguistic and religious differences between its different nations and peoples? With another, too wide-ranging junior post in the foreign affairs field, secretary of state (Africa and Latin America), there was idle, humorous speculation that the notional link, for those who had devised the combined mandate, was the prehistoric geological connection from the far, far distant past when the two continents were physically joined.

The Chrétien cabinet remained far too large for it to function very effectively as a collective, collegial decision-making body on major substantive issues. Nevertheless, the prime minister never appeared to operate with a smaller and more tractable, informal or *de facto* inner cabinet. Some senior cabinet members indeed did operate with substantial personal autonomy, most notably Finance Minister Martin because of his existing political base within the party after his unsuccessful leadership campaign in 1989, and also because of his unquestioned expertise in the top government priority of the 1990s — eliminating deficit spending and finally balancing the budget. So did some few others who had special personal ties to the prime minister, or whose portfolios were outside his areas of developed expertise or particular interest.

My conclusion was that for high policy advice and the decisions that flowed logically from that counsel, the prime minister relied even more than his immediate predecessors on his personal political advisers in the PMO. This would be supplemented, where the prime minister felt it necessary, by direct personal discussions in the case of ministers with key, functionally based responsibilities. However, in the aftermath of the 11 September 2001 terrorist attacks in the United States, and perhaps in reaction to criticism that he had responded too tardily in offering sympathy and positive support to the United States administration, Chrétien did replace his deputy prime minister, Herb Gray, with a new super-minister. Former industry minister John Manley was given responsibility for national security and the overview of all related cabinet activities — much like the charge assumed after 11 September by US Vice President Cheney.

Caucus

The government party caucus was, for many who came to Ottawa for the first time, the most interesting and vibrant representative institution during the Chrétien mandates. Political parties are not mentioned in the Constitution Act of 1867, nor in succeeding amendments to it over the years. Neither is there any comprehensive legislative scheme for the supervision and regulation of national political parties. Federal legislation touching political parties is rudimentary and piecemeal in its impact. The most important among these provisions relates to financing of political parties by way of reimbursing individual candidates as to part of their election expenses, provided that they have attained a certain minimum percentage of the actual votes cast in their constituency. The national Liberal party requires all its candidates to agree, in advance, to a transfer of part of this reimbursement to party headquarters — a practice that may be constitutionally questionable in view of the absence of any formal constitutional status for political parties, as such.

Nevertheless, political parties are the real key to the operating of the parliamentary system as constitutional law-in-action. Consequently, the absence of any formal code of conduct for the political parties, or of any really systematic monitoring of their conduct during election campaigns or in the run-up to those campaigns, including party primaries (candidate nominating meetings), represents a gap in the federal constitutional system. Contemporary constitutions — those adopted since 1945 — have tried to face up to the political reality of the presence and the effective power of political parties in the working of the democratic processes. These newer constitutional systems expressly include political parties as official constitutional players and regulate them accordingly, in conformity to general constitutional norms, including Bill of Rights-style constitutional guarantees. In Canada, the federal chief electoral officer, with only limited statutory powers, has done his best after recent elections to try to impose constitutional due process norms on the political parties. But it is a difficult operation when the ordinary courts, in their jurisprudence, still tend to view political parties as private associations that should be subject only to the ordinary, private law, and not to be regulated by the constitution or according to constitutional first principles.

The Liberal party's national caucus met once a week while the House of Commons was in session. This took place each Wednesday morning from 10 a.m. to twelve noon, immediately following on various regional and sub-regional caucus meetings. These latter could not be ignored. The BC regional caucus, including three Senators — a fourth Liberal-appointed Senator never attended — amounted to nine (and briefly ten) members during my parliamentary years in Ottawa. The Senators — Ray Perrault, Jack Austin and Len Marchand (who was later replaced by Ross Fitzpatrick) — provided us with the benefit of their experience in government, and their resulting practical skills. Perrault and Austin, during Trudeau's fourth term in office (1980–1984, when there were no Liberal MPs elected from BC), in fact had represented BC interests in Ottawa with an energy and resourcefulness that the media tended to argue was lacking under Chrétien.

The Liberal MPs from BC during the successive Chrétien mandates too often were saddled with minor governmental responsibilities, such as secretary of state or parliamentary secretary, without effective power. By virtue of these particularized responsibilities, they were constitutionally inhibited from the intra-governmental and intra-party lobbying necessary to advance and win in the caucus on issues of some vital concern to BC, such as softwood lumber or salmon conservation. Rookie MP Lou Sekora (elected in a by-election in late 1997) was left to handle the supervening "leaky condominium" issue essentially by himself. There were simply too many honorary Kentucky colonels in the BC caucus, and not enough foot soldiers to do the continuing lobbying essential to advance BC interests within caucus and in key ministerial offices.

I think we might have achieved more, as a tiny regional caucus within the much larger national caucus, with just the one BC minister.[19] This would have freed the other BC MPs to work unencumbered as a team on BC special causes. One, however, could not blame individual MPs for accepting advancement to minor ancillary governmental posts. The salary gap between MPs and Secretaries of State, for example, is vast. Nevertheless, it is known that some of the better and brighter potential recruits to the government actually refused the temptation of largely secondary, generally powerless, supporting offices.

The Ontario regional caucus, with more than one hundred Liberal MPs and a dozen or more Senators, outnumbered the BC caucus by more than eleven to one. The metropolitan Toronto sub-caucus outnumbered us by almost six to one. Once the Ontario caucus had arrived at a consensus on any major substantive policy issue or legislation, there would be, inevitably, a condition of finality to it. Ontario MPs and Senators constituted, throughout the Chrétien era, well over two-thirds of the total government caucus. Nevertheless, in the full national caucus, there was never any attempt by the Ontario MPs to impose their will, or to terminate intra-party debate. In fact, in their basic philosophy, the Ontario MPs extended over the whole political spectrum from social democrats through a large, rather soft ideological centre, to conservatives (or at least fiscal conservatives). Within the national caucus, if one raised a really interesting point and had the necessary persuasive argumentation in support of it, one could often rally

---

[19] That is to say, David Anderson, who was the BC "regional" minister in the first two Chrétien mandates, or Herb Dhaliwal, who replaced him in this capacity with the cabinet shuffle of 15 January 2002.

Ontario colleagues to speak in support.[20] The effective power was certainly there in the Ontario caucus, and it was not solely related to the numbers. It had a lot to do, also, with a will to act.

Much of the credit for the liveliness of the weekly national caucus must go to the prime minister. Except when he had to be out of town, he always attended and stayed the full two hours. On more than one occasion, when he had returned only the evening before from physically exhausting intercontinental travel, he still arrived at caucus on time. He did not preside himself, but left this function to a chair elected by secret ballot. (As it happened, the chair seemed always to be from Ontario.) The PM would arrive with a writing pad and pencil, and make detailed notes of the discussion. If the opening reports of regional and functional (status of women and the like) caucus groups were brief, and if MPs themselves were equally succinct (Senators rarely spoke), there might be enough time for up to twenty or twenty-five individual interventions. The prime minister, at the end of the session, would give a resumé of what he had heard and what he felt was important. Sometimes, he would indicate concrete action that he would take in response.

Chrétien, deliberately and observably, kept a roll of the cabinet ministers present. He indicated that he expected them to attend caucus. And this they did. It was at these national caucus meetings that he would reiterate his view that his second and third teams were of equivalent intellectual weight to his actual cabinet team. I think this was intended to bolster the morale of rank-and-file Members of Parliament. The message, however, appeared not to be lost on the members of his A team. Ministers and secretaries of state stayed the distance, from beginning to end.

Needless to say, not every caucus intervention was equally interesting or impressive in its thought content. In the early years of the

---

[20] Having served in the past as adviser to one of the most successful Ontario Premiers, John Robarts, I was asked by Ontario MPs on several occasions (and only partly in jest) to consider applying to become an honorary member of their caucus, in addition to my BC caucus status.

Chrétien government, some of the interveners would preface their remarks by too obviously obsequious praise of the leader — which the PM did not seem always to appreciate. Others rambled on. Or else told jokes — a difficult oratorical weapon in caucus, which only rare talents like George Baker of Newfoundland were capable of using effectively. The best interventions were always succinct and to the point, limited to a single issue and lasting two to three minutes, and no more.[21] I regarded the short caucus intervention, made and then repeated each week if the subject were of continuing importance and concern, to be an indispensable part of my own strategy to advance a major cause. If the prime minister made sympathetic mention of your proposal in his recapitulation, you knew you were home and could work on the conclusion accordingly.

Caucus also provided a showcase for talent within the party ranks. In the intimacy of its give-and-take, the intellectual and personal merits, as well as the shortcomings of individual Members are obvious enough, including those of ministers who, though normally not expected to intervene at all, might insist on making a statement. Our first elected caucus chair, Jane Stewart, was the scion of an Ontario political family that had already produced one short-term provincial premier and one longtime provincial opposition leader and finance minister. She was impressive in setting the intellectual tone for the new national caucus group and establishing a strong rapport between the prime minister and caucus members that carried over even after she resigned as chair to accept a cabinet post.

By general agreement and past practice, caucus meetings are "closed" — what is said inside traditionally is supposed to be treated as confidential. Otherwise, the PM or ministers of lesser importance might not want to take the risk of speaking frankly. During

---

[21] United States President Franklin Roosevelt always said it took him a week to prepare his famed ten-minute weekly Fireside Chats (national radio broadcasts), but no time at all for one-hour convention addresses.

my seven years in Parliament, there were occasional leaks to the press which the government found embarrassing. These apparently came from within the ranks of Ontario's Liberal MPs, who were sometimes sorely divided on key policy issues. In Chrétien's third term, commencing with his November 2000 re-election, breaches in the wall of secrecy surrounding caucus proceedings would become more frequent and also more deliberate, as internal battle lines were drawn within the party over the eventual succession to the Liberal leadership.

Le Chef [22]

Prime Minister Chrétien used the national caucus as part of his own personal system of checks and balances within his government and party. It was for Chrétien a potential countervail against those in cabinet with their own agendas and ambitions, who might be tempted to chart their own personal political course within the party and outside. Within caucus, and among those members from Ontario in particular, there were always divergent opinions to be found which could be juxtaposed by the prime minister against overreaching ministers should the need arise. Chrétien, who was never too inclined to favour endless speculation over philosophical objectives, instead loved the power game and the interaction of competing personalities. He was a master of this in comparison to others in the party. Of course, it generally went unsaid that the PM

[22] The special prerogatives of the prime minister were set out by Prime Minister Mackenzie King in an Order-in-Council (P.C. 3374) on 25 October 1935. It provided that only the prime minister could recommend the following: dissolution and convocation of Parliament; appointment of privy councillors, cabinet ministers, lieutenant-governors, provincial administrators, speaker of the Senate, chief justices of all courts, senators, sub-committees of council, treasury board, committee of internal economy (House of Commons), deputy heads of departments, librarians of Parliament, crown appointments in both Houses of Parliament; staff of the secretary to the governor general; recommendations in any department. In addition, but not noted by King, is the PM's right to make diplomatic appointments at the head-of-post level.

had the power (as does every other federal party leader) to refuse to sign the nomination papers of anyone within his party seeking election or re-election.[23]

In the normal course of things, however, Chrétien prided himself on his accessibility and his ability to have his staff make time for him to see any MP who asked for a personal meeting. His own office, more perhaps than that of predecessor prime ministers of either party who did not have the same deep populist inclinations, was constantly open to visiting groups of school children and others coming to Ottawa and wanting to shake hands with the prime minister and to have a photo opportunity with him. This sometimes meant his sandwiching in conversations with individual MPs in the corridors of the House, at the end of question period, or as he returned to his office one floor above the Commons chamber.

Since he also took seriously his historically symbolic role in the public company of his peers in the G-8 group, the Commonwealth, *la Francophonie,* and NATO[24] (as well as similar alphabetical organizations), his staff had him constantly on the road. Indeed, he often travelled across several continents and time zones more than once a month, returning immediately to his parliamentary duties without any break to overcome jet lag. Mixed in with this were the party fund-raising dinners which he attended, religiously, whether at one end of the country or the other. This man-in-motion schedule must have imposed severe strains on his health and well-being. The very few occasions of extreme irritation or anger in his public

---

[23] The Canada Elections Act was amended in 1970 to provide: "where the candidate has the endorsement of a registered party and wishes to have the name of the party shown in the election documents relating to him, an instrument in writing, signed by the leader of the party or by a representative designated by the leader pursuant to subsection 13(7) and stating that the candidate is endorsed by the party, shall be filed with the returning officer at the time the nomination paper is filed." The intention of this amendment was not to confer extraordinary power upon the party leaders — which it has — but to allow candidates to have their respective party allegiances printed beside their names on the ballots — something that theretofore had been forbidden.

persona tended to occur at the end of just such travel odysseys, before he could have had opportunity to readjust to Ottawa time. These rare incidents seemed to be related to the fading of his political "honeymoon" with the electorate and the media, which previously had freed him from public criticism.

Beyond the travel regimen, the prime minister also had a standard practice of having all his MPs for lunch, at 24 Sussex Drive,[25] at least once a year, usually in small groups of eight to ten to facilitate a free conversation during which none of his political aides would be present. He tended to relax at these sessions with little of the public combativeness seen elsewhere, and to touch on some of his own thoughts as to his role in public life: why he was there, and how he might be regarded in history. MPs were permitted to raise larger, long-range policy choices for the government and the dilemmas of the various policy alternatives. What was, by design, excluded were specific problem cases involving individual constituencies. These were to be raised at other times and places, beginning with the ministry directly responsible.

The Individual MP

For every major policy issue with which I was concerned, if it transcended more than one ministry, I concluded that it was necessary eventually to have the prime minister on side. This, however, would be a *subsequent* step. The first initiatives would be with the ministers responsible for the relevant file. When meeting with any minister, but particularly one in charge of a highly technical, functionally based department, I thought it advisable to be at least as well prepared as the minister and his staff. This involved research in depth if the subject were not within my pre-parliamentary expertise. I

---

[24] The North Atlantic Treaty Organization — a defensive Western military alliance formed in 1949 against the perceived threat of the Soviet Union.

[25] Originally this mansion belonged to an Ottawa lumber baron. It has been the official residence of Canadian prime ministers since 1951. Louis St. Laurent and his wife Jeanne were its first prime-ministerial occupants.

would prepare a one- or two-page brief summarizing the general problem and my own reasoned recommendations, as well as quantifying the costs if expenditures were to be involved. I also indicated the supporting documentary material that I could make available. In the subsequent meeting with the minister and his specialist staff, I normally would ask for half-an-hour at most. Where the subjects were extremely complex, technically or politically, there might sometimes be a number of such meetings extending over a period of months.

Certainly, this afforded an excellent opportunity for evaluating the executive skills of different ministers. Several impressed me. John Manley in the industry portfolio was one of these. We discussed the appropriate files and the case for federal intervention in support of funding for advanced research in science, medicine, engineering and advanced technology. Paul Martin was another. As finance minister, his support was crucial in any decision to finance the universities and advanced research institutions that were strapped for funding because of provincial cutbacks. When I met with either Manley or Martin, I would find that the minister had read the material I had given him and had done his own analysis in depth. This meant that our discussions could be concentrated on ways and means, for which the minister had his own set of questions. These were ministers on top of their departments.

I also had pleasant relations with several successive immigration ministers and, in particular, with Lucienne Robillard, who took over from Sergio Marchi in January 1996. In that I was a French-speaking MP from the West, I had volunteered to assist her in her 1995 by-election campaign in Montreal (Westmount/Ville-Marie). She had considerable prior executive experience as a member of Robert Bourassa's cabinet in Quebec, and knew the problems involved in trying to apply antique legislation developed in earlier times for problems and challenges other than those of today. But she also understood how to balance the application of the existing law in a way that would achieve public acceptance of equality of treatment for immigrants and refugees and, at the same time, obtain substantive equity in individual deserving cases. Her successor, Elinor Caplan, with previous experience as a provincial cabinet member in Ontario, struggled with the UN 1951 Geneva Convention Relating to the Status of Refugees and its 1967 Protocol.[26] Caplan's attempts to interpret, or reinterpret the rules governing Convention refugees in terms of contemporary realities often struck discord with competing forces in caucus, particularly those from Ontario. I think this explained why, after making suggestions that I thought had persuaded her on new policy directions, I would find no changes once she returned to her Ontario political base.

I had, understandably, excellent professional relations with two successive justice ministers, Allan Rock and Ann McLellan, though neither seemed as fully involved as one might have expected in ongoing federal and general constitutional questions. This amounted to an underutilization by the cabinet of expert resources and thinking within its own ranks. Our progress on the federal files and federal conflicts with Quebec and other provinces lagged accordingly.

As earlier mentioned, my *modus operandi* as MP was essentially the same in respect to each problem raised. This involved meeting with constituency interest groups directly affected; researching the problem in depth; preparing a written brief to the minister directly involved; securing a personal meeting with the minister; establishing a working consensus on problem-solving and on the balance between what we wanted to do and what we reasonably could expect to achieve; coordinating with regional groups within the national caucus; raising the issue publicly in the weekly caucus meetings; and finally, if the issue were still unresolved, seeking to raise the matter directly with the prime minister. Some of the steps would have to be repeated more than once, but it all seemed to

---

[26] The 1976 Immigration Act, which came into effect in 1978, and, as amended in 1992, applied throughout my years as an MP, established the 1967 Protocol definition of a refugee in Canadian law as Article 2(1) of the act.

work. On the TRIUMF[27] file, the whole process, to its successful conclusion, lasted about eighteen months and took, we estimated, some two hundred and fifty hours of my office's time. The financial result, as earlier mentioned, was $167.5 million for the TRIUMF project. This seemed a reasonable result for all the effort involved.

Success with TRIUMF led, logically and inevitably, to action on the larger, advanced research and education fronts. University and research institutions were suffering badly from a dearth of funding for new ventures on the leading edge of current knowledge in their fields. The immediate cause of the funding shortfall was the cutbacks in provincial financing — for which the provinces blamed Ottawa's drastic reductions in federal transfer payments. However, the facts indicated a certain difference in spending priorities between Ottawa and its provincial counterparts, with federal funds earmarked for advanced science and medicine and technology sometimes being, in Ottawa's view, diverted at the provincial level to other, quite different purposes. Beyond that, the movement to the post-industrial society and to a knowledge-based economy was setting new frontiers for advanced research which called out for national policy leadership in order to establish the goals on a nationwide basis.

In meeting with David Strangway, then president of the University of British Columbia,[28] I pointed out that while he himself frequently visited Ottawa to discuss particular projects, there were no regular meetings between university presidents as a whole and the federal departments involved in research and research funding. There was simply no systematic lobbying by the universities of the sort practised, for example, by banks and corporations, and certainly no really comprehensive communication with Ottawa about

---

[27] The TRI-University Meson Facility (TRIUMF) is Canada's largest national accelerator facility for research in particle and nuclear physics. Although located on the University of British Columbia campus, TRIUMF is a co-operative operation on the part of the Universities of Alberta, British Columbia, Carleton, Simon Fraser, and Victoria.

[28] UBC was located in my constituency of Vancouver Quadra.

what the universities and associated major research institutions were doing, or what they felt their future needs were. I suggested that the university presidents should go to Ottawa each year as a delegation to meet with the federal cabinet and with individual MPs. I also felt that university professional and teachers' associations should do the same — a practice that is now a well-publicized annual event.[29]

Within the House of Commons, an informal survey in late 1993 indicated that at least sixteen MPs, in addition to myself, had once been employed by universities or colleges. Not all of these were on the government side of the House. In addition, about fifty MPs had major advanced educational institutions within their constituencies. This meant a numerically important and potentially articulate group within the House of Commons able to make the case for direct federal support for the universities, and for arresting an evident brain drain of top scholars and researchers to the United States. While education is a provincial responsibility under the Constitution Act of 1867, a persuasive case could be made for intervention under the federal "general" power in the constitution, to meet the present "national emergency" in advanced research in science and medicine and engineering and technology and related disciplines. Besides, no province would be likely to move politically to challenge, on constitutional grounds, a purely facultative, fund-granting federal initiative — in these advanced scientific areas at least. The arts, humanities and social sciences would have to be addressed later. And so it was.

On native lands treaties, community passions — aboriginal and non-aboriginal alike — were always high. The issues were compli-

---

[29] I arranged with Dr. Strangway that I should meet with his key administrative officers each fall for a briefing on their current projects and relative priorities. We would seek to provide a liaison and additional communication with the federal science minister, and ultimately with the finance minister. When David Strangway eventually left the presidency of the University of British Columbia to take on new challenges, including advising the federal government on the best ways of allocating the new, huge special funding for advanced medical and scientific research, I was able to continue the same happy and effective relations with his successor, Martha Piper.

cated and had not always been fully explained to the public. The difficulty in achieving a consensus on desirable federal government policies, for British Columbians above all, was immense. British Columbia, unlike the rest of the country, had never had aboriginal land treaties,[30] and thus had none of the experience in patient negotiation, political give-and-take, and pragmatic accommodation already gained by all main players in the other provinces. In particular, there was confusion as to the exact constitutional status of such treaties when eventually they should be concluded with BC's aboriginal communities. What, people wondered, would be their constitutional-legal relation: (1) to the federal and provincial governments: (2) to the Constitution Act of 1867 as amended; and (3) to federal and provincial laws made under the constitution? Would, for example, the treaties, when concluded, effectively create a third level of government outside the Canadian constitution and prevail over the Canadian constitution in the event of any jurisdictional conflict?

A good deal of the confusion arose from latent ambiguities inherent in section 25 (aboriginal rights and freedoms) and section 35 (recognition of *existing* aboriginal treaty rights) of the Charter of Rights, adopted with the Constitution Act of 1982, and then amended in 1983 so as to apply also to any such rights and freedoms that might be acquired in the future. Senator Ray Perrault and I had suggested to Prime Minister Trudeau in 1980, just before the unveiling in public of the first draft of the proposed new Charter of Rights, that he should include in the Charter a provision "saving" such aboriginal rights as then existed (though without attempting to define them, which would have been impossible to achieve in the few days before official publication of the first draft of the Charter). Aboriginal rights had not been mentioned at all in the original draft, and this had seemed to us a political error of judgment. Trudeau adopted the suggestion, and sections 25

---

[30] The handful on Vancouver Island negotiated by Sir James Douglas do not detract from the general truth of this assertion; nor does the operation of Treaty No. 8 in BC's Peace River country.

and 35 of the Charter, as then published, were the result. These sections amounted, in constitutional-legal terms, to an acknowledgment of the existence of aboriginal rights — "inherent rights" in the terminology of the Indian Nations leaders of Treaty Nations 6, 7 and 8, who had asked for this affirmation in the constitution. But it was a recognition that would have to be left to future political decision-makers to spell out in terms of what those rights actually meant in concrete, secondary principles.[31]

The major confusions and difficulties over sections 25 and 35 of the Charter and their constitutional interpretation and application seem to have centered on the 1983 amendment to the Charter of Rights that included "future" rights in the categories of aboriginal rights that were to be constitutionally "saved." This amendment in 1983 to the constitution seems to have been enacted without any significant public debate or parliamentary input or attention. It was apparently conceived and put together in the justice ministry at a time of transition to a new minister, Mark MacGuigan, himself a keen student of constitutional law. After several months of direct discussions between myself and Indian Affairs Minister Jane Stewart and our respective personal staffs in the mid-1990s, and with the exchange between us of detailed drafts of the enabling legislation that was to enact the Nisga'a Treaty as federal law, a special formulation was then included by Stewart in the legislation with the prior full assent of the Nisga'a leaders. This established that the 1999 Nisga'a Treaty remains legally subject to the Canadian constitution and to the Canadian Charter of Rights and Freedoms. This stipulation might sensibly become a paradigm or model to adopt for all future BC aboriginal treaties.

Other Political Parties

People outside the political processes are often curious about personal relations across the aisle in the House. Is it possible for

---

[31] Principles that would be operational and controlling in actual problem-situations and conflicts with the countervailing constitutional interests of other main players.

government and opposition MPs to have civilized relationships, even personal friendships, in spite of the barriers that conventionally are supposed to exist because of the different philosophical or policy biases of their parties? Alex Macdonald, who was briefly CCF[32] Member of Parliament for Vancouver-Burrard during the first minority Diefenbaker government in 1957–1958, has recounted the long train journey (in the days before air travel was usual) from Vancouver to Ottawa, and the collegiality or bonding that tended to emerge across party lines among MPs on board. These were Canadian parliamentarians who all had essentially similar personal difficulties resulting from their separation from families and the maintenance of two residences (in the constituency and in the national capital), with the financial and mortgaging problems that usually went with this. I recall Pauline Jewett, who was the Liberal MP from the Ontario riding of Northumberland during the first minority Pearson government in 1963–1965, and then much later, the NDP Member of Parliament from New Westminster-Coquitlam from 1979 to 1988, commenting most poignantly on the personal and physical stresses of parliamentary work and travel. The human factor, transcending party lines, was perhaps much more present with MPs whose constituencies were far away from Ottawa, and it was no doubt accentuated in the case of Western MPs of all parties by their common feeling (sometimes described as "Western alienation sickness") of not effectively participating in national decisions that always seemed to be made in the golden triangle of Montreal, Toronto and Ottawa — for and by eastern Canadians is a fairly common view.

Then again those five-hour-plus, nonstop jet flights back and forth between Vancouver and Ottawa every week when the House was in session, threw one into regular contact with Reform MPs, as well as with the occasional Conservative Senator and the NDP members from BC. While nobody would divulge party secrets, it

---

[32] Cooperative Commonwealth Federation: socialist party precursor to the NDP.

would have been less than polite and a waste of a mutual learning opportunity not to converse on current BC interests and concerns in fisheries or aboriginal affairs or a host of other regional problems. Beyond that, many problems affecting one's own constituency could not be confined geographically, but overlapped with other constituencies and, on all rational grounds, suggested some minimum inter-party cooperation or coordination, at least in the problem-solving. There was always the issue of respecting someone else's "turf" and deferring accordingly. In my first week as an MP, Svend Robinson, the NDP member for a neighbouring constituency, phoned me to pass over an immigration file involving one of my new constituents who had mistakenly been referred to him. This was an example of the mutual courtesy extended and applied by MPs among themselves, and which I always tried to apply thereafter.

Several cases on which I worked touched the interests of Reform MP John Reynolds. One, involving the revenue ministry's imposition of the GST on condominiums on crown land leasehold developments in Hampton Court, within my constituency, appeared to parallel similar problems in Reynolds' West Vancouver constituency. He got in touch with me after reading a progress report on this matter in my quarterly riding newsletter. I kept Reynolds fully informed thereafter, up to and including the successful resolution of the problem through my own direct negotiations with the federal revenue and finance ministers. Another file touching Reynolds concerned a TRIUMF employee facing extradition to the United States. Thirty years before, as a young, anti-Vietnam war, college student activist, this man had been convicted in New York on a minor drug possession count. He had escaped to Canada, where, under an assumed name, he had built a respectable professional and community life, and had married a Canadian citizen. When his identity was finally revealed by an informer, his extradition was sought by the US authorities. Some of this man's TRIUMF co-workers brought his plight urgently to my attention. In consequence, I took up his case directly with New

York's Governor Pataki, and also sought the intercession of US Congressman Amo Houghton from New York State. It was only then that I discovered that, although this man worked in my constituency, he actually lived and voted in Reynolds'. I immediately informed Reynolds of what I had done to date. He asked me to continue. Of course, I kept him advised up to the final, successful conclusion of this case.

On the key, controversial West Coast fishery issues, I was officially charged with these files for a period in my capacity as parliamentary secretary to the minister of fisheries. Indeed, even after I had moved from fisheries to become parliamentary secretary for foreign affairs, I continued to speak in the House on various fisheries issues. In the course of all this, I had discussions from time to time with the Reform fisheries critic, John Cummins, and his party colleagues, whose views I passed on to the government in hope of finding consensual approaches to the problems involved. Conservative Senator Pat Carney was also extremely helpful with advice and information drawn from her own past work on the fisheries files as a minister in the Mulroney government. John Fraser, a personal friend of long standing, also volunteered lessons from his own rich experience as fisheries minister.

Non-Elected Senate

Over several decades of testimony, as an invited expert witness on federalism and the Canadian constitution before a number of different royal commissions, parliamentary joint committees, Senate special committees, as well as provincial royal commissions and legislative committees, I had been asked, most frequently of all, for advice on how to replace the presently purely appointive Canadian Senate with some form of elective body; and also as to what form and what competences any new, elected Senate should have. There was general agreement at every level that a non-elected legislative chamber had, by definition, no political legitimacy today. It was a constitutional anachronism received from nineteenth-century

Britain and out of touch with contemporary community attitudes and expectations in Canada. The members of the present Senate evidently share many of these public misgivings and doubts as to their role. By a consciously exercised politic of self-restraint, the Senate majority has accepted that, except in quite extraordinary circumstances, it should refrain today from rejecting bills coming to it from the House of Commons, or from subjecting them to crippling amendments not envisaged by the original drafters. And this, even though, apart from money bills, the Senate's legal powers under the Canadian constitution as written are essentially the same as those of the House of Commons.

This self-denying ordinance of the Senate usually has been exercised, in modern times, with fine sensitivity and judgement and with the attempt, always, at discussion with representatives of the House of Commons and on obtaining agreed, consensual, negotiated solutions on points the Senate majority at any time might feel needed improvement in pending legislation. One might sometimes conclude that many government MPs, if not necessarily the government's House Leader in the Commons, were not unhappy to have the Senate impose delay on any bill considered to have been rushed through the House of Commons on not altogether convincing arguments of urgency. This may have been what happened with the bill on unification of Newfoundland school districts, which raised historical, religion-based issues not resolved to general satisfaction in the earlier Commons debate. It may have happened as well with the bill enacting the Nisga'a Treaty into federal law. Within a few years of its 1993 election victory, the Chrétien government, through attrition of Senate membership and the exercise of its own constitutional monopoly on filling vacancies in the Senate, had secured a Liberal majority in the Upper House. But enough Liberal Senators in that majority sometimes have been prepared to exercise the political independence conferred by their unassailable legal tenure (until mandatory retirement at age seventy-five) to risk embarrassing their own government by refusing to jump to the command of the Commons leadership to ratify immediately, without full debate, politically controversial or questionable bills.[33]

Another area in which the Senate, even with a Liberal majority, has been disposed to exercise independence from the government, has been in the working of its committee system. In the House, the imperatives of government leadership are more apparent in their operation since they are usually less subtle or diplomatic in their application. The *raison d'être* of the committee system (and the incidental justification for the remarkable absence of both government and opposition MPs from the House sittings, outside the one-hour question period each day), is that it is in committee where reasoned debate and give-and-take between government and opposition parties over government legislation is supposed to take place. Before the change made by House vote with the help of fifty-six dissident government MPs in November 2002, committee chairs were designated by the government whip and ritualistically elected by the government majority. In consequence, they often seemed to view their function, whether on constitutional grounds or for reasons of political prudence, as being something akin to that of parliamentary secretary as an unquestioning defender of government interests at all costs. This may help account for the evident failure of the House committee system to achieve anything approaching the functional efficacy of the legislative committees in other contemporary liberal democratic constitutional systems. Senate committees, however, with much less for their members to anticipate in the way of future government favours, have seemed always to exercise a greater freedom.

---

[33] In situations of majority government, the House leadership sometimes yields to the temptation to be arrogant in imposing its own agenda, timetable and time allocation for debate, before using the government majority to impose closure. Interparty negotiation is supposed to produce agreed, consensual regulation of the mechanics of House business. The several separate incidents in the second Chrétien mandate (1997–2000), when opposition parties in the House — the *Bloc Québécois* and the Reform party — in quick succession compelled marathon all-night sittings, reflected an irritation not wholly confined to opposition ranks when this process failed.

Further, with a more leisurely personal agenda — since the Senators are free from the need to prepare for re-election every few years — Senators seem to choose the committees on which they are to serve with some greater regard than MPs for the relevance of their own professional background, experience, education and training. Further still, and perhaps because of an extra degree of financial affluence, Senators don't seem so ready to queue up for committees offering frequent foreign travel or other like perquisites. Senate Committees reporting on financial, banking and business issues normally achieve a very high level of technical expertise. This may not be so surprising, considering that expertise in these particular areas usually turns up in the resumés of many Senators. But in areas such as foreign affairs or defence, where no such obvious disparity in terms of areas of personal knowledge or experience should exist between the members of the two Houses, the Senate committees, in usually hearing the same witnesses and passing on the same evidentiary material as the House committees, seem able to come up with much clearer or politically less inhibited conclusions. An example might be the House and the Senate committee reports, within a few weeks of each other in the year 2000, on the then recent NATO armed intervention and aerial bombardment of Yugoslavia (in which Canadian armed forces participated). Peter Stollery (an ex-MP), chair of the Senate committee, and its bipartisan members deserve high marks for a report that cut through conflicting testimony to focus on the key issues of the decision by the Canadian government to bypass the UN security council and the general assembly, and the legal authority they could have provided, in favour of NATO-based military air strikes.

The case for an Upper House in Canada — particularly an Upper House that is to be reformed into a directly elected chamber — is strengthened by the Senate's work in its own committees. Substantial changes (which have yet to be made) to the House of Commons committee structures, however, could no doubt counter this in the future. The argument here, of course, is directed to only one of the traditional grounds advanced by constitutionalists for having an Upper House. It is that it will function as a chamber of "sober second thought," examining and, where patently necessary, recommending and imposing corrections and amendments to bills too hastily drafted or adopted by the Lower House. The other traditional argument for retaining a Senate in Canada is that it is, far more than the House of Commons, a "regional" chamber in which representation is geographically weighted so as to afford special protection to cultural diversity and to linguistic, religious and (in the United States Supreme Court's phrase) "discrete and insular" minority interests not otherwise effectively defended in the Commons.

Historically in Canada, the Senate as a "regional" chamber has often been seen to have a special responsibility for maintaining the "French fact" in its various political-constitutional formulations, whether "two founding nations," or some other "special" or "particular" constitutional status for Quebec within the Canadian federal system. This "regional" chamber aspect of the Senate's constitutional personality has not been particularly apparent in recent times, perhaps because of the political facts-of-life of the operation of the constitutional appointment system of Senators. There are no obvious representatives of Quebec nationalist, separatist forces in the Senate today, only Liberals, Conservatives, a few independents, and a single ex-Conservative who now claims Reform-Alliance allegiance. Nevertheless the "French fact" or "Quebec fact" has operated, decisively, by way of negative implication for all attempts to reform the Senate and to transform it from a purely appointive body to some form of popularly-elected chamber. This relates to the disproportional balance in Senate membership (which was essentially established with the original Constitution Act of 1867), which today gives Quebec twenty-four Senators out of a total of one hundred and four — and leaves late-entry British Columbia, which joined confederation in 1871, with only its original allotment of six Senators. And this notwithstanding the recent rapid increase in BC's population and economic importance in relation to Quebec and the rest of the country.

Attempts to correct this regional imbalance in Senate member-ship now run into the constitutional hurdle, under section 42 (1)(c) of the Constitution Act of 1982, that they can only be effected by the difficult constitutional amending processes established under article 38(1) of the same act — namely, by Senate and House reso-lutions, accompanied by similar resolutions of the legislatures of at least two-thirds of the provinces, including either Quebec or Ontario. Attempts to surmount this particular constitutional hur-dle have included the Charlottetown Accord formulae, whose political solution was to guarantee Quebec, for all time, twenty-five percent of the representation in the House of Commons, and this notwithstanding any supervening changes in population distribu-tion, as the price for readjusting regional numbers in the Senate. But tampering with the generally accepted constitutional principle of representation by population as the primary basis for constitut-ing a Lower House was not calculated to win popular approval. This was one of the compelling political arguments used to defeat the Charlottetown Agreement in the 1992 nationwide constitution-al referendum held by the Mulroney Conservative government on that accord.

The Pepin-Robarts Task Force had raised another possible way out of the dilemma by in effect introducing the principle of a nec-essary "concurrent majority" in the Senate on any bill from the House of Commons affecting Quebec's fundamental concerns (i.e., the primacy of the "French fact" and of the French language and culture within Quebec). This principle (with some debt to early nineteenth-century, Southern US statesman John Calhoun) would have required a majority vote by the Senate as a whole, but including a separate — concurrent — majority vote of the Quebec Senators, in favour of any measure already passed through the Lower House touching the "French fact" in Quebec. Some sort of compromise, along these lines, might be what would be politically required in the future to break the constitutional deadlock over redressing the current marked regional imbalance in representa-tion in the Senate, unless, of course, another total revision of the constitution (including the Senate) were to be ventured upon,

Charlottetown Agreement style. It is for this reason that many who would wish to modernize the Senate by providing for the election of its members have finally opted for "last resort" remedies such as abolishing the Senate altogether (although any such measures would run into their own constitutional hurdles under the detailed formulae for constitutional amendment set out in the Constitution Act of 1982).

Over the years, my own various substantive proposals for reforming the Senate amounted, in sum, to electing Senators by direct, popular vote; with equal representation, on a five-region basis, throughout Canada; but limiting any such elected Senate to a suspensive veto only (a one to three months delay at most) on any bills passed by the Lower House. In addition, I had suggested that such a reformed Senate have the constitutional power to examine and review (though not necessarily to defeat) all treaties signed by Canada and all order-in-council appointments (nomination of judges to the Supreme Court of Canada and all federal courts; appointment of provincial lieutenant-governors; appointment of ambassadors and senior diplomats, deputy ministers, heads of crown corporations and similar federal agencies). The other major constitutional competence appropriate to any such reformed, elected Upper House would be a general supervisory, investigatory power in relation to federal government operations. The Senate could thereby take over what, too often, has been prudently consigned by the federal executive to overly expensive and inevitably foot-dragging royal commissions.[34]

---

[34] The Pepin-Robarts suggestion for requiring a "concurrent majority" must inevitably arise when the issue of fundamental reform and passage to a direct, popularly elected Senate comes up for public debate in the future.

II

———

WESTMINSTER PARADIGM
AND OTTAWA PRACTICE

When the new Parliament assembled in Ottawa following the 1993 election, the cabinet had already been appointed by Prime Minster Chrétien. The preamble to the Constitution Act of 1867 speaks of a Canadian "Constitution similar in Principle to that of the United Kingdom." Perhaps in the full historical spirit of the original Westminster model, the announcement of the formation of the new cabinet should have waited on the convening of Parliament. In contradistinction to systems like that of the United States, where there is a complete constitutional separation of the executive and legislative arms of government, the British and Canadian cabinets are parliamentary executives, responsible *in the end* to their respective Houses of Commons, and with their maintenance in office dependent at all times on majority support therein. In the modern experience of both Great Britain and Canada, however, where majority government is almost invariably the electoral outcome, deference to constitutional courtesies such as that indicated above is considered politically irrelevant and unnecessary.

Speaker's Office

The first task of the new House of Commons was to elect its presiding officer, or Speaker. By tradition and practice, this appointment had always been seen as the personal prerogative of the prime minister[35] — sometimes as a consolation prize for someone left out of cabinet, sometimes as a highly decorous final promotion for someone preparing to retire from politics. It had twice, in the cases of Roland Michener and of Jeanne Sauvé, proved a dignified stepping-stone to the office of governor general (appointment to which, as earlier noted, also effectively falls within the personal prerogatives of the prime minister). There had been a fairly consistent practice of alternation of the speakership between Quebec and the other provinces. The first and, so far, only female appointee was Jeanne Sauvé (1980–1984).

In September 1986, Prime Minister Mulroney, in an apparently politically guileless gesture to the spirit of parliamentary democracy, decided to turn the whole process of selecting a speaker over to the House of Commons. Members of Parliament, both government and opposition, would elect their speaker by secret ballot rather than automatically ratify the government's choice, as had been the practice since confederation. In this first such instance of a free election, the presumed first preference of the prime minister was defeated by another government party MP, former fisheries minister John Fraser. Fraser had been backed in the secret balloting by opposition MPs, as well as by a considerable number of government MPs who clearly sympathized with him in the circumstances of his earlier resignation from the Mulroney government, when he had accepted the political blame in a classical, West-

---

[35] See fn. 22, p. 43.

minster-style display of ministerial solidarity for the government's lapses in the so-called "tainted tuna" affair.

For the new House, elected in October 1993, the selection of the speaker by secret ballot was again followed. In this instance, however, a procedure was introduced which appeared to be designed to eliminate the slightest suggestion of cabinet coercion or favouritism. The name of every MP would remain on the ballot paper unless directly removed by the individual MP, himself or herself. A number of the newly elected members — my colleague Anna Terrana from East Vancouver and myself among them — decided to leave our names in. This was mainly out of curiosity about the actual working of this free election system rather than in expectation of lasting beyond the first ballot.

Although, as expected, I was quickly eliminated, I was quite happy that I had done this. The official opposition *Bloc Québécois* party, and the Reform party invited me, before the actual balloting, to meet with their respective caucuses to outline what I thought the role of the House of Commons and its speaker should be in a fully contemporary constitutional system. The leader of the opposition, Lucien Bouchard, personally introduced me to his MPs. I spoke to them for over an hour, including questions-and-answers. I think the caucus was surprised that, as an MP from Western Canada, I spoke fluent French, even though Bouchard had first reminded them that I had taught at the *Sorbonne,* the *Collège de France* and other metropolitan French institutions, as well as at Laval University. He also noted that I had advised several Quebec premiers of different parties.

I had a similar pleasant experience with the Reform party. Deborah Grey, who had served in the preceding Parliament as her party's first elected MP, introduced me to their caucus. And Preston Manning, the Reform leader, referred to my constitutional writings during our session. This opened the way to future interesting and informal exchanges on constitutional and other issues with opposition party MPs throughout my first term in Ottawa. I saw myself participating in an experiment in a new approach to parliamentary processes that had been inherited from the late nineteenth century, when British parliamentary government was at its highest development. This was completed for me when I was then invited by the new Liberal party caucus chair, Jane Stewart, to address the government caucus as if I were one of the other, more serious candidates for the speakership. Again I talked about what I thought the House of Commons should become, as well as what the potential role of the speaker might be in any rationalization and modernization of this venerable institution.

The actual election in 1993 paralleled that of John Fraser seven years before. In our case, Chrétien's presumed favoured candidate, Jean-Robert Gauthier (later a Senator), lost to another government MP who was supported by the key opposition parties. But this took five ballots. The two leading candidates were in an electoral dead-heat after the first couple of rounds, the result only being determined when a government MP had to leave the House before the final ballot had taken place. Of course, the outcome may have turned, in the end, on personality factors rather than issues of philosophy of government. The prime minister's assumed first choice, who had been opposition whip under John Turner, had the richer knowledge of parliamentary history and practice. The opposition parties and some government MPs may have preferred the more down to earth approach of the eventual victor, Gilbert Parent. Of course, there was also the obvious opposition enjoyment in embarrassing the government. Interestingly, in 1997, when Parent ran for re-election as speaker against John Nunziata, the former dissident Liberal MP who now sat as an independent, he was understood to have won again by only a single ballot.

As the new speaker in 1993, Gilbert Parent clearly lacked the full background in constitutional and general legal history of his predecessor, John Fraser, who had always been able to assert an extra personal authority in his constitutional-legal rulings. Speaker Parent, on the other hand, had been a school teacher and principal in his pre-parliamentary career. He was, by nature, a very kind man, who, rather than invoke the law of parliamentary custom and

▲ *Nomination supporters at the end of a come-from-behind victory, at 1:00 a.m., March 24, 1993. Steve Bosch 1993/The Vancouver Sun*

▲ *Ted McWhinney with Prime Minister Jean Chrétien*

▲ *With my predecessor as MP for Vancouver Quadra, John Turner*

▲ *With Frank Murphy, mainstay of the Liberal party in Vancouver Quadra*

▲ *1993 Quadra team, with Jim Paloubis and Thomas Braun*
(joint campaign managers — Elizabeth Murphy absent), and a
young-looking leader of the opposition, Jean Chrétien

▲ *With broadcaster Hanson Lau, NDP MLA Jenny Kwan and Wayne Lee*

▲ *Being sworn in as a Member of Parliament 1993, witnessed by my former student, David Kilgour MP for Edmonton-Southeast, and the Clerk of the House of Commons, Robert Marleau*

▲ *House of Commons debate — surrounded (clockwise from right) by Dan McTeague,*
Brenda Chamberlain, Lyle Vanclief, Herb Dhaliwal, Raymond Chan,
and the late Shaughnessy Cohen

▲ *With Dr. Eric Vogt, former TRIUMF director, alongside commercial compact cyclotron*

▲ *With UBC Nobel laureate, Biochemist Michael Smith*

▲ *With UBC president David Strangway at Ottawa reception, 1997*

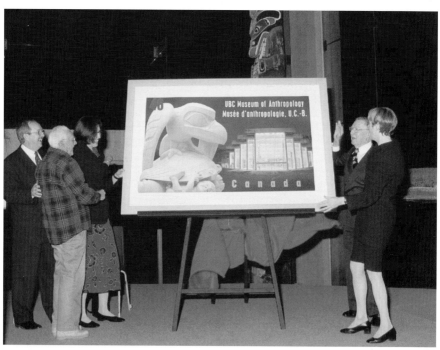

▲ *With UBC president Martha Piper unveiling the Canada Post stamp commemorating Haida artist Bill Reid at the UBC Museum of Anthropology, 1999*

precedent, tended to rely on friendly persuasion. When a contested issue arose during House proceedings, he preferred to defer any definitive decision in order to refer the matter to his professional Commons staff. This usually meant a delay of several days, which sometimes allowed partisan passions to cool. However, it also meant an often rather discursive written opinion, containing conclusions that didn't always flow logically and inevitably from the technical-legal argumentation advanced in the text. It was nonetheless sufficiently acceptable, in most cases, to the opposition parties, allowing for accommodation without too much political loss of face on either side. One's impression was that Speaker Parent's main interest was in solving immediate problems amicably in order to get on with House business without too much fuss, rather than trying to chart new parliamentary law and practice for an aging institution.

The office of speaker, of course, had inherited a much larger problem — what authoritative scholarly critics, as diverse as British jurist George Keeton and Nobel-laureate political economist Friedrich Hayek, had identified as the "Passing of Parliament." By this, they meant the general decline of the legislative arm of government because of the very complexity of community decision-making in the emerging post-industrial society. The critics pointed to the proliferation of administrative law and regulation and the inevitable delegation of authority to a new class of skilled bureaucrats and technocrats. These particular civil servants, their ideas and techniques, would be beyond the comprehension or effective control of elected parliamentarians whose thinking and talents had been so largely formed and shaped in the image of the classical, nineteenth-century British House of Commons.

The corporal's guard of MPs present in the Commons each day, before and after the televised question period, is a consequence of the felt necessity of MPs to get back to their offices to study particular files in depth, or to try to make something at least out of the Commons committee processes. But it also reflects a deep sense of frustration as to inherited parliamentary processes that no longer respond to the reality of contemporary lawmaking. That is to say, how decisions are actually made today: the law-in-action, rather than the abstract law-in-books. Earnest suggestions have been advanced from time to time from para-parliamentary study groups in Ottawa and elsewhere, for reform of the parliamentary committee system. Proposals have been made for paying a special salary bonus to Commons committee chairs — an additional $11,000 per year was the figure floated around during my second term as an MP.

The more radical proposal, recently adopted by MPs (including, as earlier noted, fifty-six rebellious Liberals) against the wishes of the Chrétien government, was to have a secret ballot of committee members to select their committee chair, so as to overcome the present system whereby the government whip in effect selects, and the government majority in the committee concerned automatically ratifies that choice. Unfortunately, this change will touch only superficial elements in the institutional system, and will not in any serious way affect the underling problem of constitutional balance marked by the decline of the legislature and the burgeoning of the executive arm of government.

Question Period

The office of speaker has no constitutional capacity to effect any fundamental restructuring of executive-legislative institutional relations, or, indeed, to introduce new constitutional checks and balances within Parliament itself. Speaker Parent at least tried from the chair to change the tone and style of question period. Question period remains the focal point, in a public relations sense, of the House of Commons — something accentuated over the last quarter century or so by televising the proceedings of the Commons. Speaker Fraser had terminated the old practice of MPs rhythmically banging the lids of their desks as a means of signaling their approval of their spokespersons in question period. The desk banging had been roundly condemned by many people watching parliamentary exchanges from the visitors' galleries or on their home television screens as schoolboy antics that brought the institution into public disrepute. However, the new indices of partisan approval — repeated and prolonged "standing ovations" and the wild applause and laughter that often accompany them, even for purely banal verbal sallies — seem hardly much improvement.

Speaker Parent's own favoured response to any form of disorder was to get up from his chair, thereby automatically shutting down the House's electronic system (microphones, amplifiers, simultaneous translation, etc.). He would remain standing, sometimes for several minutes, until things calmed down, then try to resume House business. He was especially gentle with newcomers who strayed over the line. This was evidenced in his decision not to take disciplinary action against new *Bloc* MP Stéphan Tremblay (successor to Lucien Bouchard in the riding of Lac Saint-Jean, and the House's youngest member at the time), who, in a theatrical, symbolic protest against a perceived failure of the government to act on youth and student issues, physically removed his chair from the chamber.[36]

Parent, however, appeared rather tired and disillusioned toward the end of his second term. The MPs elected in 1993 seemed politer and more deferential to the chair, as well as more respectful of the House as an institution, than the class elected in 1997. This, no doubt, was because of the high idealism of the 208 first-time Members in 1993. When, in October 2000, Prime Minister Chrétien announced yet another early election, Speaker Parent chose the final day of our sitting to inform the House that he would not be running for personal re-election as an MP.

Parent's successor, Peter Milliken, was elected speaker in January 2001 after several ballots (yet again with strong opposition support). A lawyer from Kingston, Ontario, with a deep knowledge of British parliamentary precedent and practice, Milliken was

---

[36] I had myself written to Speaker Parent suggesting that the parliamentary offence here, if any, should be treated as venial and not substantial.

possessed of a rare and welcome oral and written literary elegance. Consequently, he inspired hope for some imaginative reinterpretation of old parliamentary constitutional rules and precedents to meet the rather different community needs and expectations concerning Parliament at the opening of the new century. It would take a brave speaker, however, to take on the challenge of reforming question period.

Question period has moved rather far from its original intention and purpose of eliciting public information on government policies and their practical application and execution in concrete cases. Certainly, this function could be attempted more systematically and scientifically today by following the example of congressional committees in the United States, or even continental European models, where research staff and independent counsel are provided on a nonpartisan basis to government and opposition alike. Something might also be done by way of the speaker exercising his powers over House internal procedures and allowing a free sweep to the television cameras so that they can record the totality of the Commons activities.

As it is, question period preempts too much time of leading MPs and their staffs — time which might be better employed in studying pending legislation. For example, I often observed the *Bloc Québécois* caucus leaders beginning their preparation for that day's question period at 7:30 a.m. over breakfast in the Centre Block cafeteria. On the opposition side, this involved reviewing staff-prepared research files, trial-and-error testing of possible questions, rehearsing oral presentations, anticipating (by "informed guesses") government replies, and developing possible rejoinders for follow-up supplementary questions. This would go on right up to the beginning of question period at 2:00 p.m.

Of course, I followed a similar schedule on those occasions when, as parliamentary secretary, I took the absent minister's place in fisheries or foreign affairs. I would begin my question period "war games" about 10:00 a.m., and proceed, with occasional departmental expert briefings, to rehearse trial "mock" answers. This was the *régime* that existed on the government side of the House, enjoined and supplemented by the legion of political aides and ministerial civil servants available to the ruling party.

Committees and the Party Whip

One learns, immediately upon arrival in Ottawa, the power of the party whip and of the House Leader, government or opposition as the case may be. By long-tolerated practice, the allocation of offices in the various buildings of Parliament — whether in the strategically placed Centre Block or the much more elegant and spacious West and East Blocks, or in the distant Confederation Building — is made by the whips of the respective parties. As a matter of parliamentary law, however, this is a function that properly should be divided between the Commons and Senate speakers as part of their historic prerogatives.

The respective party whips, and not the speaker, also decide on the seating of MPs in the House of Commons: *who* should sit *where*. The power represented by this decision, in terms of its political and electoral importance, was vastly enhanced when it was decided to televise House proceedings and debates. The fixed camera rule, as enforced by the speaker (but representing a consensus among party House leaders), establishes a few narrow, permanent viewing corridors for the House television cameras. Understandably, they are focused on the prime minister and his senior government colleagues and on the opposition party leaders. This creates some highly prized seats within effective camera range that can be viewed by nationwide tv audiences.

Seating allocation within each party is supposed to occur according to seniority of first election to the House. This is clearly followed for the range of ministerial and paraministerial posts. There is, however, a margin of discretion and subjective choice available as to all the remaining posts (such as parliamentary secretaries), and much resulting irritation at any perceived preferential treatment or mistreatment. It is widely assumed that the party whip favours those MPs who, in the heat of question period, are more overtly enthusiastic in leading standing ovations, or in applauding attempted sallies of wit (or ridicule of opponents) by colleagues.[37]

Some members, with a passing irreverence for House custom which decrees that MPs, to be recognized by the speaker, must remain in their pre-allocated seats, operate as "migratory birds," rushing to occupy the choice, television camera-friendly seats of absent ministers, etc. This practice was frowned upon, but neither the speaker (who would have had the necessary constitutional power) nor the whip (who had the political power) was disposed to do anything about it. Just before the House was dissolved in fall of 2000, the government whip yielded to entreaties for choice seats (with assured television-camera exposure) from two Conservative MPs who had just quit their party for our ranks. This caused some ill-feeling among the displaced government MPs, who wondered aloud if these last-minute political converts were worth the cost of having the whip change the accepted "rules of the game."

Much more substantial as a practical demonstration of the discretionary powers and favours exercised by the House Leader and the whip, is the disposition of committee assignments and, until recently, of the key appointments as committee chairs. At the start of a new session, MPs in each party are circularized by their whip to determine their committee preferences. The extraordinary turnover of MPs in the 1993 election meant that there were a large number of vacant committee seats to be filled. While the seniority rule had a certain relevance, the opportunities for "grace and favour" discretion in the making of these appointments were legion.

One quickly learnt, by trial-and-error if not by referring to House folklore, which committees were to be sought after and which to

---

[37] In my own service as parliamentary secretary, successively in fisheries and then in foreign affairs, I happened to be placed behind the prime minister in the direct angle of television camera vision. I was struck by the resulting degree of public recognition that I received outside the House.

be avoided. There was ferocious lobbying for membership on committees whose mandate could be construed as warranting frequent travel to interesting foreign destinations at government expense. More than one committee chair would complain privately about the "passengers" from all parties, who had to be taken onto his committee because of binding assignment from the respective whip's offices, but who had little or nothing in the way of specialized expertise or knowledge (or even interest) to offer.

Apparently in deference to notions of constitutional separation-of-powers within the government itself, neither committee chairs nor the ministers in charge of the departments to which a committee's mandate relates are normally consulted as to the MPs assigned to these committees. This particular criticism seems to be leveled most frequently at committees such as foreign affairs and defence. By comparison, the more strictly functionally oriented committees such as fisheries and aboriginal affairs have often done rather better in attracting genuine specialists and other MPs directly interested in the large, continuing problems of these ministries. Finance, transportation and justice, although limited essentially to Canada in their travel, have a certain home-constituency prestige, and usually attract a professional element to their membership.

It is the party whip, in any case, who makes the committee choices, by balancing seniority of service and the usual "cabinet" criteria (gender, ethnicity, region, and the like) against "good behaviour" within the party. Certainly, I was troubled when the committee of which I was chair was employed as a form of parliamentary purgatory for several MPs who had disobeyed the whip's call and had not voted in the House on a particular motion. I think it had something to do with the then (as now) controversial gun control bill. Consequently, they were transferred to my then low-key, apparently non-controversial and certainly non-travelling committee, from their original committee assignments.

As it happened, the particular committee to which these presumed "delinquent" MPs were sent for "purification" was the joint standing committee of the Senate and House of Commons on the Library of Parliament. It had been dormant for a number of years, but had been revived after the 1993 election. When I was first offered the post of co-chair of this committee,[38] my thought was that I was being consigned to the world of letters that I had left behind. But I accepted, and immediately found that, so far from being a merely honorific post, my committee would have to deal with two major and pressing problems: finding a new parliamentary librarian, and overseeing the Library's transition into the informatics era. So much was becoming electronic in contemporary communications that the research needs of today's parliamentarians could no longer be served adequately by a classical library, no matter how rich the collection of books and other treasures it had built up over the past century and a quarter.

The post of parliamentary librarian had, apart from its professional/technical charge, the politically sensitive responsibility of supervision and direction of the highly sophisticated parliamentary research staff available to all committees, political parties and MPs. On enquiry, it became clear that this librarian post — one of high stature in Ottawa, with commensurate emoluments and tenure — might not turn on strictly professional qualifications. Apparently, there were several nonprofessional candidates-in-waiting, one of whom was reputed to be a defeated federal Liberal with significant political backing.

I concluded that, in the period of historical transition in which the Library of Parliament now found itself, it would be vital to maintain its rich, accumulated heritage of books and the classical reading room facilities that had grown around this, but, at the same time, to embrace the new information technologies. To do both, of course, would require major additional funds in a period of extreme budget austerity. I also concluded that we should have a fully trained professional librarian in charge. The best qualified

---

[38] The other co-chair, by the protocol governing Senate-House committees, would be a Senator.

candidate was the excellent deputy librarian, Richard Paré. There was a full consensus on these key issues in our fine, and exceedingly well-read, all-party committee.[39]

In interventions in the national caucus and also in direct communication with Finance Minister Martin, I made the case for special funding for the Library of Parliament to enable it to enter the electronic age without having to cut back on its traditional services or to sell off any of its historical collections (including the famed Audubon first editions) to pay for the cost of transition. Paul Martin agreed, and that part of the battle was won. I also wrote to the prime minister, recommending Paré for the post (appointment to which remained within the PM's prerogative powers). When Paré was subsequently appointed, I decided that my mandate, as committee co-chair, had been fully discharged. Of course, it was the unexpected assignment of those delinquent MPs that bothered me still as being out of character with the nature and responsibility of my committee. Consequently, I arranged, quietly, to resign both as co-chair and member of the committee. The essential work had been done. It was time to move on to other challenges.

The whip for each party in the House also designates persons to be nominated for foreign travel as members of various informal parliamentary friendship groups that are officially recognized by the speaker's office, and therefore fully financed from a special fund maintained and administered by the speaker's office. The subjective element in the choice of MPs and Senators designated for these delegations is much more manifest than with the regular House committees. Indeed, certain individual parliamentarians turn up with noticeable frequency on these foreign travel tours. Foreign ambassadors, as well as some Canadian ambassadors, have voiced quiet misgivings from time to time about the intellectual

---

[39] A happy feature of this committee for me was the membership of Senator Dick Doyle, who, as editor of the *Globe and Mail*, had published my first articles on the Canadian constitution and federalism.

weight and seriousness in the membership of these delegations. For this reason, many serious-minded parliamentarians refrain from seeking inclusion in them. Preston Manning, as Reform party leader, tried (not with complete success) to influence his MPs to exercise self-restraint in accepting such invitations.

One particularly useful committee, however, was the Canada-United States joint parliamentary committee. Perhaps because its travel was limited by definition to the two countries involved, those who chose to take part in it each year would normally be drawn by the subject matter and the concrete problem-solving opportunities that it opened up. It turned out to be a high quality operation on both the Canadian and the American sides, with particularly able and dedicated, long-serving Canadian co-chairs in Thunder Bay–Superior North MP Joe Comuzzi and Toronto Senator Jerry Grafstein. It is surprising that, with the ever closer Canada-US legal ties and cooperation in fiscal, economic and trade matters since the conclusion of the bilateral agreement on free trade, no serious attempt has yet been made at the constitutional level to accord this relationship some more permanent parliamentary-constitutional form.

The party whip has one further important function, occasionally implemented with flair and imagination by the younger, politically appointed, salaried staff attached to the whip's office. That is, to select the MPs who would present the party policy viewpoints in the regular debates on government legislation, or would ask that day's questions, or would make the one-minute declarations that are permitted during question period. While elements of favouritism inevitably enter into these allocations, the overriding considerations are public credibility, mastery of the subject matter, and individual comfort with the televised proceedings of the House.

An often difficult part of the exercise, on the government side, is the need to provide some television exposure to the more junior ministers, including secretaries of state. Not all of these persons are blessedly articulate or comfortable with their government assignments. One solution has been the planted question prepared

in the government party secretariat. This exercise is often banal
enough to provoke laughter on the other side of the House, and
might well be discarded for that reason. Some of our more inde-
pendent-minded MPs refuse to pose these often rather silly questions to government ministers.

Unlike the one-hour question period, where the House, on
both sides, is invariably crowded, the regular debates usually take
place before a rump group of members, no more than a dozen or
even half a dozen, covering both government and opposition. The
opposition at times is unkind enough to call for a quorum (twenty
members including the Speaker), at which point the House must
suspend its operations while the quorum bells are rung until the
magic number of members appears,[40] however briefly, before disappearing again. If relations across the aisle happen to be cordial,
there is a common interest in turning a blind eye to the mass of
empty seats in the House. By agreement of all parties, the fixed,
narrow range of the television cameras prevents their sweeping
around the House to highlight Members writing letters, reading
newspapers, chatting with colleagues, or snoozing. More particularly, this avoids focusing on empty desks. Consequently, the viewing public accords the thrusts and exchanges of parliamentary
debate a degree of credibility which they otherwise would not have.

In fact, however, the debates occasionally display a high standard
of individual research, reasoning, and argumentation. Certainly,
every party secretariat has salaried speech writers who can turn
out, quickly, canned briefs, varying slightly in literary style, that will
make their party's case on any issue. This is sometimes embarrass-
ingly obvious when an MP, at short notice, takes the brief and
delivers it without opportunity for advance reading. These canned
presentation often seemed to have been written with satirical
humour on a takeout-order basis by retired civil servants. They
were too often replete with standard schoolroom clichés like "We

---

[40] If this does not happen within fifteen minutes, the Speaker will adjourn
the House until the next day.

stand on guard," "Canada is a country with frontiers on three oceans," "True north strong," and the like. This was especially marked with fisheries ministry speech writers, but I think the functionaries there had been too often disappointed in the past in the performance of government MPs in debate, and had concluded that they must set their literary standards somewhat modestly. I always asked to see these canned briefs in advance of speaking, in order at least to confirm the basic elements of the party's current policy positions on any subject, but I never actually used them. I made my own interventions based on my own personal notes. Among others on the Government side who would never read the canned briefs but made their own addresses: John Bryden, Charles Caccia, John Godfrey, Derek Lee, Clifford Lincoln, Dan McTeague, Dennis Mills, Peter Adams and Peter Milliken. Among the francophone members, one should cite Bernard Patry. Carolyn Bennett, who for a time was chair of the women's caucus within the Government party, would usually liberate herself from the pre-prepared briefs and speak her own opinions.

III

—⁓—

OTHER PLAYERS

The constitutional-institutional roster remains to be completed by identifying other key players of varying degrees of relevance today as constitutional law-in-action. One of these, the office of titular head-of-state (the Queen, governor-general, and provincial lieutenant-governor) has "received" British imperial roots that were of some substantive legal importance in the historical period before the Imperial Conference of 1926, the enactment of the Statute of Westminster in 1931, and the emergence of full Dominion status and sovereignty within the then British Empire and Commonwealth. A second institution, the Supreme Court of Canada in its contemporary projection as a *de facto* constitutional court also has British constitutional antecedents in the Judicial Committee of the Privy Council, which functioned as a final appellate tribunal until the abolition of its jurisdiction for Canadian cases by the Canadian Parliament in 1949.[41] A third institution, the political party organization, is para-constitutional in its nature and origins, and has remained, until very recently, outside the scope of constitutional review and regulation.

Titular Offices

The Constitution Act of 1867, in providing for the devolution of self-government to Canada within the then British colonial empire, reflected its own legal origins as a statute of the British Parliament when it proclaimed that "The Executive Government and Authority of and over Canada is hereby declared to continue and be vested in the Queen."[42] While that statement has long since ceased to reflect the constitutional facts-of-life and constitutional law-in-action in Canada, residual, symbolic elements are still to be found today in contemporary Canadian legal documents. Thus section 41(a) of the Constitution Act of 1982, sponsored by Prime Minister Trudeau, stipulated that the "office of the Queen" can only be amended with the assent of both Houses of Parliament and all the provincial legislatures. The monarchy, unlike God and the institution of private property, had not been an issue of controversy, or even discussion, during the long round (1980–1982) of federal-provincial intergovernmental negotiation on Trudeau's constitutional patriation package. It was simply not a priority issue.[43]

This is not to say that such acceptance of the status quo with regard to the Queen's office had always been the case. Indeed, in the early years of the "quiet [and sometimes not so quiet] revolu-

---

[41] There are now some latter-day, major, non-imperial borrowings and influences on the Supreme Court of Canada, particularly from the United States.

[42] Part III, Executive Power (Sections 9–16).

[43] This may seem surprising considering that another "old" Commonwealth federal system, Australia, with its predominant Anglo-Saxon component in comparison to Canada, held a referendum in the mid-1990s on the constitutional question of abolishing the monarchical ties and becoming a republic. This proposal probably would have secured popular approval as a

tion" in Quebec, the continuation of the monarchy in Canada became a matter of considerable political issue. The final volume of the Pearson memoirs records a most revealing, pre-luncheon conversation between Her Majesty and the then Canadian prime minister at Buckingham Palace in November 1967: "On her own, she brought up the question of the monarchy in Canada as something which would, before long, have to be examined in depth. She was very anxious that the monarchy, or any controversy over it, should not be prejudicial to Canadian unity or a source of division. I was moved by her attitude and her sensitive understanding of the changing situation, and I talked with her along the lines of my discussion with Michael Adeane." In his earlier discussion with Sir Michael Adeane, the Queen's secretary, Pearson records that he had suggested to Adeane that it might be "better to abandon these constitutional fictions" relating to the Queen as the sovereign of Canada, "and to consider the Queen as the sovereign of Britain, which she is, but also as Head of the Commonwealth, which she also is, rather than an absentee monarch endeavouring, though with grace and dignity and charm, to live up to a designation which is theoretical rather than exact."[44]

Of course, nothing came of these royal and prime-ministerial musings. Nor did anything come of Prime Minister Trudeau's apparent attempt in 1972–1973 to convince the Queen to agree to a five-point plan to turn Canada into a presidential republic.[45] It would appear that Trudeau decided that any public controversy over this wasn't worth the political bother. The question of

---

constitutional amendment except for disagreements on the secondary issue of whether to select the resulting head-of-state by indirect election or by direct popular vote.

[44] John A. Munro and Alex I. Inglis, eds., *Mike: The Memoirs of the Right Honourable Lester B. Pearson, Volume 3, 1957–1968* (Toronto: University of Toronto Press, 1975), 300–301.

[45] According to documents released in January 2003 by the British Public Records Office, as reported, not in the Canadian press, but in a piece on 9 January 2003 by Sergey Borisov in the Russian newspaper *Pravda*, from a report originating with *Agence France Presse*.

abolishing the monarchy seems hardly likely to arise again for serious discussion during the reign of the present Queen. Separatist
leaders in Quebec have made clear that if and when "sovereignty-
association" for Quebec should be attained, Quebec would seek to
remain a member of the (British) Commonwealth of Nations and
would, as such, have no difficulty in accepting the Queen's titular
role as "Head of the Commonwealth."

André Ouellet, a highly pragmatic Canadian foreign minister
who became head of Canada Post, was happy to approve a very late
request from some of my constituents in Vancouver Quadra for a
special postage stamp in honour of the Queen Mother's one-hun-
dredth birthday on 4 August 2000. His staff produced, in record
time, a postage stamp that was a colour symphony in yellow and
rose. It was officially unveiled in the monarchist fortress of Victoria, BC, before a euphoric crowd (median-age eighty-plus)
representative of that older generation of Canadians who had
developed special ties with the royal family during World War II —
in particular with the present Queen's father, King George VI, and
her mother, the late Queen Mother Elizabeth.

When the present Queen dies or decides to retire, there might
be a political issue as to a successor in relation to Canada. If a future federal government, in these circumstances, should decide to
make a final symbolic, constitutional-legal break with the monarchy, it is likely that this would be done by constitutional indirection
— seemingly absent-mindedly, by simply failing to proclaim any
Canadian successor to the former monarch. All this, of course, has
to do with constitutional folklore, and not the day-by-day reality of
the concrete constitutional order that we have had in place in
Canada since the British Parliament's enactment of the Statute of
Westminster which effectively recognized, for public international
law as well as constitutional law purposes, the sovereignty and
independence of Canada as an international person in its own
right. This devolution and transfer of power was made freely and
in good will by London with no backward glances into history. It
is certain that the British government would display a similar
grace and absence of rancour in regard to any latter-day symbolic

gestures that a Canadian government might wish to make in cutting its last monarchical ties.

Some casual controversies can still arise over the purely ornamental accessories or trappings of the monarchical connection, however — and this without any fault or responsibility on the part of the British government. The adoption of the "Nickle Resolution"[46] by the Canadian House of Commons in 1919 ended the granting of both titular and nontitular honours to Canadians. These, until that time, had been made in London on the recommendation of the Canadian government. Prime Minister R.B. Bennett (1930–1935) restored the practice of titles, but Prime Minister Mackenzie King, on taking office again in 1935, reinstated the prohibition.[47] Canadians were reminded of the no-titles rule when Prime Minister Chrétien successfully blocked British Prime Minister Tony Blair from recommending to Her Majesty the appointment of then Canadian press magnate, Conrad Black, to the British House of Lords.[48] In contrast, two recent Canadian prime ministers, John Diefenbaker and Pierre Trudeau, were named, without any public fuss, to the high British civil award, Companion of Honour (CH), and a third, Mike Pearson, received the even more prestigious Order of Merit (OM). Appointments to both of these orders remain within the Queen's personal disposition.[49] More inconsistently perhaps, given our proud no "foreign titles"

---

[46] W.F. Nickle was the Conservative (Unionist) MP for Kingston.

[47] Sir Ernest MacMillan, the long-time conductor of the Toronto Symphony Orchestra, was one of the last Canadians to be knighted before Mackenzie King stopped the practice.

[48] Lord Black was able, finally, to achieve his ennoblement in 2001 by bypassing Chrétien and Canada. He opted for British citizenship, renouncing that of the land of his birth in the process.

[49] Mackenzie King's renunciation of titles for Canadians in 1935 proved no impediment to the creation of autonomous Canadian honours. Prime Minister Pearson's initiative to create an Order of Canada was soon followed by key provinces — Quebec, Ontario, British Columbia and others — in establishing their own provincial orders. As an MP, and as a private citizen before my election, I was frequently asked to write letters in support of particular candidates for such awards, and I was happy to do so.

egalitarianism, Canada still abounds with organizations — charitable, artistic and the like — which by letters-patent carry the prefix "Royal."

What is more, many hundreds, perhaps thousands of Canadians bear the title "Honourable" for life by virtue of their having been federal ministers (or even junior secretaries of state), Senators, Supreme Court judges, provincial lieutenant governors, and by a strange and obviously contrived special arrangement, part-time directors of the Canadian Security and Intelligence Service. A record of sorts is apparently held by a Newfoundland MP, who served as a minister for only two weeks, but would remain "Honourable" for the rest of his life. The official justification for this practice in Canada, at least for federal politicians, relates to membership in the Privy Council of Canada. But this is an arcane medieval office that has largely lapsed even in Britain. It has been dead in Canada, in all but its name, since the nineteenth century. It would make good sense, if this title is to be retained, to limit its employment to actual tenure of the public office, so that it is lost to the individual when he or she ceases to hold that office.

Within Canada, and except for the occasional official visit, the Queen's titular role has by now disappeared. On the occasion of her fiftieth golden jubilee visit to Canada in October 2002, Queen Elizabeth, signally, was not invited to perform the honorific and purely formal function of reading Prime Minister Chrétien's speech from the throne opening the new session of the Canadian Parliament. That task was performed instead by the governor general acting, as usual, as Canada's titular head-of-state. By the middle of the twentieth century, the titular head-of-state role of the governor general had atrophied to the point where, except for the rare situation of a minority government, or the even rarer event of a revolt against a prime minister within the government party, the once great constitutional powers of this office might be said hardly to exist at all.

The discretionary, prerogative powers once exercised by the crown in Britain itself had withered away with the onset of repre-

sentative democratic government based on universal adult suf-
frage. And so also has it been in Canada, with the discretionary,
prerogative powers that the office of the governor general "received" from Britain. The elaborate formal definitions of those
powers in the Constitution Act of 1867 are simply out-of-date, as
are the constitutional conventions and practice of the Victorian
age. However, because changes in social attitudes have been recognized in a timely enough fashion, and then acted upon through
an equally timely politic of constitutional self-restraint and benign
inaction, the office of governor general (like that of the monarch)
is hardly a political priority for constitutional change today. Besides, the office has begun to take on another and rather different,
non-political orientation in keeping with developments in other
countries in modern times. If a concert pianist could become president of newly independent Poland after World War I, a playwright
president of the post-Communist Czech Republic, and literate
scholars the heads of state for Ireland and for India, why not follow
the same course for Canada? The extra step of entirely emancipat-
ing the titular head of state from the taint of political appointment
would be to provide, as elsewhere, for some form of election by
Parliament or the people.

Section 41 of the Constitution Act of 1982 prescribes that any
amendment to the constitution touching the office of the governor general (like that of the Queen and the lieutenant governor)
requires resolutions of the two Houses of Parliament and of the
legislatures of *each* of the provinces. But there is nothing within the
ambit of the prime minister's prerogative powers as they now exist
to prevent him or her from submitting the name of any proposed
appointee to a purely Canadian office to the House of Commons
for the prior approval of MPs. With the designation of a provincial
lieutenant governor, the prime minister, if he so wished, could
choose to refer the name of a proposed appointee to both the
House of Commons and to the legislature of the province concerned, or to the legislature of that province alone, prior to his
acting on the appointment. Once established, it is difficult to

conceive that any subsequent government would retreat from such a practice.

Some might fear that the extra-constitutional legitimacy flowing from the vote of the federal or provincial legislatures might encourage a self-confident titular head-of-state to try to repeat what Australian Governor General Sir John Kerr did when he literally threw out the majority Labour party government of Prime Minister Gough Whitlam in 1975.[50] The constitutional winds of change, however, have decreed that any further such attempted exercises in prerogative powers by a governor general would be based on false precedents that properly belong in the dustbin of constitutional history. It is not, in any case, a difficult or time-consuming job to draft and adopt a legislative definition and limitation of the governor general's or lieutenant governor's role and remaining discretionary powers — something that could be achieved by simple federal legislation as part of the constitution.

Over the last fifty years, there exist only a handful of cases — all relatively minor — in federal or provincial constitutional practice in Canada, where the question of the historical reserve, prerogative powers of the governor general or of a provincial lieutenant governor has arisen. At the federal level, in February 1968, the Pearson minority government was defeated on a nonsubstantive financial measure. Despite some calls for resignation of the Pearson government by those who hadn't studied the evolving British parliamentary precedents from the 1920s onwards, the leader of the opposition, Robert Stanfield, declined to press any partisan political advantage by campaigning publicly for the government's resignation (and in the process create a bad constitutional precedent). No issue for the governor general therefore arose. In 1979, Prime Minister Joe Clark, himself leader of a minority government, lost a snap vote in the House on a minor budgetary provision.

---

[50] In 1926, Canadian governor general Lord Byng of Vimy denied minority Prime Minister Mackenzie King's request for a dissolution of the House, but the constitutional significance of his action is less clear cut.

Clark, however, decided, notwithstanding the 1968 example, to re-quest a dissolution from the governor general. Governor General Schreyer appears correctly to have had some doubt — which we are told he conveyed to Clark — as to whether a dissolution was constitutionally necessary or even appropriate, so far as defeat on a nonsubstantive financial measure was no longer considered a "confidence" issue. Consequently, he did not immediately grant Clark's request, but suggested reconsideration. Clark returned to his Centre Block office, where Schreyer telephoned him a short time later to agree to dissolve Parliament. (Clark was defeated in the ensuing general election.)

In 1997, after only three and a half years of his statutory five-year mandate, and again in 2000 with a similar amount of time remain-ing in the statutory life of Parliament, Chrétien requested an early dissolution of the House of Commons, although he had not been defeated on any confidence or budget vote, and had no apparent constitutional-legal grounds on which to base his request for dis-solution. On much earlier, imperial, pre-Statute of Westminster constitutional precedents, the governor general would have been fully entitled to reject this request, and no doubt would have done so. But not so at the end of the twentieth century. Dissolutions were granted in each case, and Chrétien won re-election.

At the provincial level, in 1991, the lieutenant governor of British Columbia, David Lam, brokered an intraparty succession in the then ruling Social Credit administration of the province, when incumbent premier Bill Vander Zalm lost the apparent support of his party caucus, although no defeat or actual vote had occurred in the legislature. Since the Social Credit government had a majority in the legislature and since its caucus remained cohesive in public, the lieutenant governor felt constitutionally able to indicate that he would accept the person designated by the government caucus as now commanding its support, and would act accordingly. There was therefore no question of granting the premier a dissolution or of calling upon the leader of the opposition to try to form a gov-ernment. A peaceful transition within the government then occurred, with the old premier being replaced by a new premier from the government party caucus. This was achieved without political bloodshed or any need for dissolution in a highly pragmatic and elegant, and also creative and fully constitutional employment of any residual discretionary powers of the lieutenant governor. The old premier, after meeting with the lieutenant governor, went along gracefully with the transition. His successor, however, lost the next general election, including her own seat in the legislature.

In Ontario, the Conservative government of Frank Miller lost its majority in the 1985 general election, but still remained the largest party in the legislature. Before the new legislature came into session, however, the two opposition parties, the Liberals and the NDP, indicated to their province's lieutenant governor, John Black Aird, that the NDP would guarantee the Liberal party majority support in the legislature for the next two years. Without waiting for the legislature to be convened so as to have the incumbent Conservative premier face the House, which would have been the normal practice under the old, imperial constitutional precedents, Ontario's lieutenant governor, in a wholly contemporary but also (in my own view, as expressed at the time) creative constitutional interpretation, commissioned Liberal leader David Peterson to form a government. (Premier Peterson's minority government went to the people in 1987 and was returned with a large majority.)

The above provincial constitutional precedents indicate that there may be still some remaining margin of discretion which the titular head-of-state has available, but that it must be used with high pragmatism and common sense, and with full regard also to the political reality today of the practical limitations on the power of a purely nonelected official vis-à-vis popularly elected legislative majorities. At the federal level, the most recent constitutional practice shows full deference by the governor general to the views of incumbent prime ministers on questions relating to the dissolution of the House. This has been so even in cases where, in the past imperial era, the governor general would have felt free to make his own prerogative decisions and to ignore his first minister's advice for a dissolution; or where, in a kindly exercise of his wisdom and experience, he might have counseled the prime minister to act otherwise in the prime minister's own political best interest.

In the prolonged crisis in the national Liberal leadership in 2002, resulting from internal caucus dissidence over Jean Chrétien's apparent decision to continue as party leader and prime minister up to or even during the next general election, references have been made to the role of Lieutenant Governor Lam in the intraparty succession to the premiership in British Columbia in 1991. Conflicting versions of the constitutional precedent involved were put forward. There was also suggestion for joining the 1991 BC case to the 1985 Ontario practice to form a new and more comprehensive precedent on constitutional succession to the prime-ministership. In this particular interpretation, if a number of MPs on the government side of the House sufficient to break a prime-ministerial majority were to communicate their common position to the governor general, it should be enough to warrant withdrawal by the governor general of the prime minister's mandate to govern. This interpretation would be, I suggest, a misreading of the 1991 BC precedent. A sufficient number of MLAs within the BC government caucus were able to demonstrate, to the satisfaction of the lieutenant governor, that they were able to command a clear majority within the legislature as a whole, and not merely within the government caucus. Such a situation, self-evidently, would not be present in the hypothetical case cited above. Conceivably, a change of government might be brought about if one or more of the opposition parties would be prepared to demonstrate, to the satisfaction of the governor general, their commitment to support the government party dissidents in numbers sufficient thereby to produce a firm majority in the House. This has yet to happen, of course.

By the same token, however, an alternative hypothetical scenario that would have a prime minister request, and have the right to receive, a dissolution of the House as a means of disciplining party dissidents to keep them in line in the House, would seem an unacceptable exercise in the titular head-of-state's reserve, prerogative powers. The titular head-of-state's constitutional obligation is to ensure a stable, continuing government able to command the support of the House, but not to cross the constitutional line and become a politically activist Warwick-the-King-maker.[51] The reserve powers, to the extent that they continue at the present day, have to be understood and applied in this light.

The constitutional attrition of the powers of the governor general was once linked to the fact that the incumbents of the office, in unbroken sequence until after World War II, were all non-Canadian. It would be inelegant, to say the least, in the interpretation widely advanced after the Byng-King constitutional conflict of 1926, for a non-Canadian to exercise sweeping discretionary powers against a popularly elected prime minister and government of the day. This particular point of view lost much of its original force when the last British governor general, the accomplished World War II military leader, Viscount Alexander of Tunis, who had commanded Canadian troops during the Allied campaign in Italy, was succeeded by the first Canadian governor general, Vincent Massey. The objections to the governor general's discretionary powers and their exercise would have to be rested, as they then were to become, on the purely appointive, non-elective character of the office — the argument that constitutional legitimacy must derive from popular election, which is the objection advanced also against the Senate today.

The Canadian appointees to the office in the post-World War II era have almost invariably had prior federal parliamentary or civil service experience. Vincent Massey, a leading Ontario Liberal, had served briefly in Mackenzie King's government in 1925 before being appointed the first Canadian minister to Washington,[52] 1926–

---

[51] Richard Neville, Earl of Warwick (1428–1471). Prime Minister Diefenbaker, who had read deeply in early English constitutional history, was known to decry Warwick's skills when attacking his own intra-party opponents.

[52] Canada did not have diplomatic representation in Washington above the rank of minister until Leighton McCarthy was made ambassador in July 1944.

1930, and high commissioner to London, 1935–1946. General Georges Vanier not only had a record of distinguished military service in World War I, but an equally distinguished diplomatic service in World War II. Roland Michener and Jeanne Sauvé had served as Speakers of the House of Commons. Edward Schreyer and Ray Hnatyshyn and Romeo LeBlanc had all served as MPs and in cabinet posts, federal or provincial. The latest incumbent, Adrienne Clarkson, had no such "federal" qualifications but, instead, formidable attainments in communications and the arts which imply a new emphasis in the search for a governor general on persons who can interpret and define the new Canadian cultural pluralism and who may also reflect it in their own distinctive contributions.[53] The office is now closer to the general population. The resplendent court dress, originally prescribed for those who were not entitled to wear military dress uniforms, is now essentially relegated to the museums. The officeholder emphasizes communicating with people on every possible public occasion and seeking to project, in public addresses, his or her own particular vision of the new Canada.

Constitutional Court

Contrary to much general opinion, even in academic and professional legal circles, a constitutional role for the Supreme Court of Canada did not begin with the adoption in 1982 of the constitutionally entrenched Charter of Rights and Freedoms. From the adoption of the original Constitution Act of 1867, Canadian courts, including the Supreme Court of Canada after it was established in 1875 as the highest Canadian internal appellate jurisdiction, had

---

[53] I have known four of the recent lieutenant governors of British Columbia. Their selections — again within the prime minister's personal prerogatives — reveal the same patterns as recent choices for the post of governor general: the distinguished soldier from the Italian campaign in World War II, Henry Bell-Irving; the community leader and benefactor, David Lam; the skillful and graceful inter-governmental negotiator, Garde Gardom; and the former MP and federal cabinet minister, Iona Campagnolo.

always been subject, as earlier noted, to appeal from their judge-
ments to the Judicial Committee of the Privy Council sitting in
London. This final colonial court of appeal, a somewhat informally
structured tribunal composed of up to seven judges recruited for
the occasion largely from members or former members of the
highest British domestic courts, was the final appellate tribunal for
the British colonial empire. Its mandate, in that capacity, was to
ensure conformity with British general law applying to the colonies
overseas and also, in measure, with British private law, of laws
adopted by colonial legislatures and decisions of colonial courts.

In its imperial heyday in the late nineteenth and early twentieth
centuries, the Judicial Committee of the Privy Council had
produced a significant amount of case law jurisprudence on the
Canadian constitution, in cases mainly involving the division of
legislative powers between the federal government and the provinces under sections 91 and 92 of the Constitution Act of 1867.
Indeed, it distinguished itself, over this period lasting about a half
century, by a consistent embrace of provincial rights ideas, favouring the provinces at the expense of federal power. The decentralizing, centrifugal emphasis that the Judicial Committee gave to
the original Constitution Act of 1867 reflected something of a
"deux nations" conception of the constitutional compromises that
had led to its adoption (and affirmed a felt concern for Quebec's
historical special status within the federal system). The key expo-
nents of the decentralizing approach to the Constitution Act of
1867 were two Scottish jurists (and philosophers), Lord Watson
and, after him, Lord Haldane, who sat on the successive Canadian
cases for most of that period.

But strong criticisms of the consequences, as law-in-action, of
the Watson-Haldane jurisprudence for the Canadian federal system, advanced in the 1920s and 1930s by Anglo-Canadian jurists,
including W.P.M. Kennedy, Frank Scott, Vincent MacDonald and,
in later years, the young Bora Laskin, had begun to produce some
political second thoughts in Canada, paralleling the constitutional
events set in motion by the Imperial Conference in 1926 and the

adoption of the Statute of Westminster in 1931, and the evolution of full Dominion status and Canadian sovereignty and independence within the new British Commonwealth of Nations.

The retirement of Lord Haldane and the appointment of a new Lord Chancellor, Lord Sankey, a brilliant intellectual jurist in his own right, but one who more readily accepted Keynesian economics and the centralizing imperatives of the 1930s, allowed for a new centripetally oriented jurisprudence from the Privy Council's Judicial Committee, and a conscious favouring of the federal government in sections 91 and 92 conflicts between federal and provincial power. The Canadian Parliament in 1949 formally abolished appeals from Canada to this judicial vestige of empire. By this time, the Supreme Court of Canada, now promoted as final appellate tribunal for Canada, was firmly established in the new, centralizing jurisprudence recognized by Lord Sankey.

In 1949, the Supreme Court of Canada, logically and inevitably, also assumed the function of judicial review of the Canadian constitution. What is less generally known, however, is that the Supreme Court, in its own right, had already begun to develop a substantial constitutional civil liberties jurisprudence — and this on what was, initially at least, a rather flimsy legal foundation: the expression, in the first paragraph of the Preamble to the Constitution Act of 1867, of a "Constitution similar in Principle to that of the United Kingdom." Chief Justice Duff and Justice Cannon, in the *Alberta Press* case in 1938, made this a foundation for incorporating, from British domestic law, the celebrated concept of the Common Law rights of Englishmen, first formulated by the leading English constitutionalist of the nineteenth century, Albert Venn Dicey.[54] The idea was taken up throughout the decade of the 1950s by a brilliant and articulate group of liberal Supreme Court judges, led by Mr. Justice Ivan Rand, who extended the concept

---

[54] Dicey saw it as the product of the ordinary decisions of the ordinary private law courts of the land in the English constitutional battles of the seventeenth and eighteenth centuries, which postulated freedom of speech and freedom of the press as elemental legal rights of citizenship.

of constitutionally protected common law liberties in Canada to cover the classic spectrum of freedom of speech and expression, assembly, press and publication, and what might be called a protection of elemental procedural due process and fairness in executive administration. These rulings were made in cases originating with a particular litigation-oriented, religious proselytizing group, the Jehovah's Witnesses. I remember writing, at the time, that the Jehovah's Witnesses had given Canada a bill of rights, and it was a historical judgement soon taken up by others.

The Canadian judiciary was rather cool, almost disdaining, of Prime Minister Diefenbaker's attempt to concretize all this judicial achievement in his 1960 Canadian Bill of Rights, adopted by the Canadian Parliament in the form of an ordinary statute. Diefenbaker did this because he feared insurmountable provincial opposition and delay if he attempted to pursue the existing political route to constitutional amendment in Canada. There followed a prolonged inactivity in approaching the issue of constitutionally protected political rights until Trudeau's constitutional project was launched in 1980 with its key component of a constitutionally entrenched Charter of Rights.

The Supreme Court of Canada judges evidently were not consulted in advance as to the nature and content and styling of the new Charter. Nor were they aware, as they arguably should have been, of the profound consequences of its adoption for existing constitutional institutions, and above all for the Supreme Court itself.[55] A veritable constitutional revolution in executive-legislative-judicial relations was effected with the adoption of the Charter as part of the Constitution in 1982, one for which neither the cabinet, Parliament nor court was adequately prepared. The Supreme Court of Canada, predictably enough, was transmuted into a form of *de facto* special constitutional court, but with none of the institutional safeguards and inbuilt checks and balances that have given parallel institutions in the United States and Europe a certain con-

---

[55] For that matter, the political leaders who drafted and approved the new Charter appear not to have considered fully its implications for the Supreme Court.

stitutional legitimacy, as well as a large degree of operational efficacy in community problem-solving on concrete tension-issues.[56]
In the result, and in its decisions on high political *causes célèbres,* the
Supreme Court of Canada, since the constitutional changes of
1982, is too often accused of rushing in where even angels (and
certainly the constitutional courts of other mature countries)
might more prudently choose not to tread, and of never accepting
the principle and practice of judicial self-restraint as a necessary
corollary to inclinations to judicial lawmaking. For those who have
accepted the inevitability of judicial legislation in the interstices of
judicial interpretation, which can never be reduced to a "pure,"
logical process, the democratic corrective of some more public
involvement in the processes of selection of judges for the court
would seem a timely and useful reform to make.

Para-Constitutional Players

Political parties are not mentioned in the original Constitution Act
of 1867, nor in the various amendments and additions to it over
the years, including the Constitution Act of 1982. The absence
from the BNA Act of 1867 is not surprising, nor even the omission
from the Act of 1982 which, apart from "patriation" proper and
the new constitutional amending machinery, was concentrated in
its substantive provisions on the new Charter of Rights. Contemporary constitutions, of which the German (Bonn) Constitution of

---

[56] The paradigm *de jure* (European) or *de facto* (USA) special constitutional court is characterized by several distinct elements not present in its contemporary Canadian analogue. The first of these is *constitutional legitimacy* in
the sense of election of its judges for a defined term of years by the national
legislature (European paradigm); or at least ratification of executive nomination of judges by one of its legislative chambers (United States paradigm).
Second: *specialization,* in the sense that its judges invariably will be chosen for
nomination and elected on a basis of demonstrated specialist expertise in
constitutional and administrative law. Finally: *collegiality,* in the sense of
accepting as a prime obligation to supply a clear, common and agreed statement of majority consensus in any case, and to function as a team — an
orchestra, and not a collection of solo performers — even while retaining
the right to file separate or dissenting opinions.

1949 has become the paradigm and a favoured model for new constitution-makers elsewhere, do specifically include and define
political parties in their basic charter. These new constitutional systems also have essayed a systematic, principled review of the internal organization and practice of the political parties, as well as of
the operation of national electoral laws to ensure full access to voting rights and the removal of any unnecessary clogs to the political
processes.[57]

Canadian courts have lagged well behind United States and
European constitutional courts in the monitoring of the internal
party political processes and general electoral processes so as to
make them accord with notions of democratic representativeness
and equality, and also elementary fairness and procedural due
process. This is less due, I think, to any unreadiness on the part of
the judiciary to accept contemporary ideas of constitutionalism
than to an absence of concrete litigation on which to fashion new
jurisprudence. Canadians have simply lacked the will or inspira-
tion to go to the courts to vindicate their democratic rights in these
areas, and there has been a dearth of the public interest advocacy
organizations that one finds in the United States and elsewhere
ready to research and then to finance constitutional test cases. The
political parties themselves have their own internal judicial tribunals to which complaints can be made on grounds of alleged
violation of the political parties' own legal charters and constitutions, and through which corrective action can be sought and
obtained. This, however, is not a substitute for a definitive legal
ruling by courts of law. It lacks, outside the political party itself, the
sanctions attending to court decisions. It also misses out on the

---

[57] The seminal idea behind this judicial watchdog role over the political
parties and the electoral laws comes from a celebrated dictum by Mr. Justice
(later Chief Justice) Harlan Stone of the United States Supreme Court, pronounced in 1938, elaborating a positive responsibility for the courts to keep
the general political processes free and unobstructed. So much of the US
constitutional principle of the separation of powers and the mutual checks
and balances that must operate between executive, legislative, and judiciary
if the constitutional system is to operate properly is posited upon a constitu-

public educational side since the internal party rulings attract very little media attention, or the sort of editorial comment that might guide and help correct political party conduct for the future.

In my own nomination contest in Vancouver Quadra in 1992–1993, I discovered the problem of antique Liberal party rules that allowed every constituency association to supplement its ranks by a further twenty-five percent of nonresidents who could, literally, be brought in from distant corners of the province. Even worse, as a newly arrived candidate for nomination, I discovered that candidates already in the field had used their time to sign up nonresidents in numbers well over the twenty-five percent quota, who were banked up in preferred priority waiting lists. This meant that if my supporters should sign up, say, four hundred new members, we would, thereby legitimate the addition to the constituency association rolls of one hundred nonresident members already signed up by other candidates. Needless to say, this caused us some dismay. Should we challenge this twenty-five percent nonresident quota — at least in its standard application through the preferred priority waiting lists — and if we challenged, should we do it through the party internal appellate process or go directly to the courts? In the end, we decided that we should fight it out in the constituency association electoral processes, flawed as these might be. This we did, with a successful nomination campaign that is now considered a paradigm within the Liberal party of late-entry, come-from-behind, electoral strategic design. I, however, had agreed that if we should lose, we would take the constitutional route, through the judicial process and seek a declaratory judgement

---

tional basic norm of representative democracy. By 1944, the US Supreme Court had already rejected the distinction, stemming from its earlier, post-Civil War jurisprudence, that political parties were purely "private" as opposed to "public" organizations and therefore immune from constitutional review and control by the courts. After some brief judicial hesitation in 1946 in extending and applying judicial control over political parties and the electoral processes more widely and concretely, this Court, in a detailed series of cases thereafter put aside the "political questions" argument as any bar to judicial review on these issues.

from the courts outlawing the twenty-five percent nonresident gap, and its attendant glosses, on constitutional-legal grounds. At the same time, I indicated that, as part of any such judicially based approach, I would confirm that I could not myself be a candidate for party nomination in any new constituency association ballot that might be decreed by the courts.[58]

One curious aspect of the parallelism — it is sometimes an antinomy or direct contradiction — between the party organization outside Parliament and the party caucus within Parliament and especially in the elected House of Commons, was brought into the open in the internecine conflicts within both arenas — party organization and parliamentary caucus — in the bitter civil war that divided the national Liberal party throughout 2002–2003 over the issue of party leadership. This is a euphemistic way of describing the debate over whether the party organization, in convention, could and should compel the prime minister to retire by designating a leadership review under party rules, and organizing a hostile majority in the resulting internal vote by party delegates. Over the time period 2002–2003, and even before, there have been intensive battles within constituency associations throughout the nation to elect the constituency executive slates that would ultimately choose those who would determine the outcome of essential convention votes on these issues.

The United States-style national party convention has much to commend it in terms of the public interest and attention that it attracts. The gathering of some thousands of delegates elected by party organizations in all the states of the Union in order to designate by their vote in convention their party's candidate for the presidency of the United States certainly focuses media attention on party personalities and policies in the election year. In addition,

---

[58] After the 1993 constitutional embarrassment, the federal Liberal party organization, on legal advice from Frank Murphy, closed the constitutional gap by abolishing the twenty-five percent non-residency eligibility, retaining only a "grandfather clause" to permit longtime constituency members to opt to continue membership notwithstanding loss of residency through the decennial electoral boundary redistributions.

giving party workers a public role in the electoral process helps build up enthusiasm for the ultimate campaign, which must rest very heavily upon legions of these political foot-soldiers. The first such convention in Canada was that of the Liberal party in 1919,[59] at which Mackenzie King emerged victorious over Nova Scotia's W.S. Fielding. King, of course, had experienced American political conventions first hand during his years as a labour relations expert working for the Rockefellers in Chicago after his defeat in North York in the Canadian general election of 1911. There would not be another Liberal leadership convention until 1948, when King's handpicked successor, Louis St. Laurent, triumphed over Saskatchewan's Jimmy Gardiner. The leadership convention system works easily and logically in the United States, with its constitutional separation-of-powers, in which the president is completely divorced, constitutionally, from the legislative arm of government — the Senate and the House of Representatives. However, it has always had the potential to operate strangely when artificially engrafted upon a "received" British system of parliamentary executive.[60]

The public statements made by Liberal MPs and extra-parliamentary officials during the party's internal conflicts of 2002–2003 often displayed a misunderstanding of basic constitutional-legal rules. There were suggestions that the governor general might be persuaded to take official notice of extra-parliamentary events in arenas like the national party convention, and to move to exercise her residual, discretionary, prerogative powers accordingly. The constitutional reality remains, however, that unless and until any decisions or votes in a national party convention should actually be translated into concrete action within the parliamentary caucus

---

[59] Earlier, Wilfrid Laurier had organized a very successful Liberal national policy convention in Ottawa in 1893.

[60] Under the Constitution Act of 1867, there is no constitutional-institutional separation of powers. The prime minister is a Member of Parliament and dependent, in constitutional terms, for his continuance in office as prime minister upon his being able to command a majority of votes in the House of Commons.

itself, there would be no new constitutional "facts" of which the governor general could properly be seized.

Dissidence within a national party organization, mounted into a successful revolt within that organization, would have to be paralleled by similar action within the House itself, and would be constitutionally irrelevant and nonreceivable in itself. To warrant withdrawal of a serving prime minister's mandate, the governor general would have to have had demonstrated in empirically based terms that the prime minister could no longer command a majority in the House. This could come from a House vote. Alternatively, it could come, on the Ontario provincial precedent of 1985, from a numerical sufficiency of government and opposition MPs communicating to the governor general in writing or in some other tangible, objectively verifiable form that they would commit themselves to some other designated candidate for that office. These are difficult but necessary constitutional tests to require, of course, but the displacement of any head-of-government is also a very serious step. The president (titular head-of-state) of India has followed a practice similar to the Ontario provincial precedent in recent instances of no-clear majority general election results. Certainly, this could sensibly be applied federally in Canada if the political situation should arise here.[61]

---

[61] It is, however, a misreading and misunderstanding of the BC lieutenant governor's role in the succession in the provincial premiership in 1991 to imagine any capricious exercise in vice-regal free will. BC Lieutenant Governor David Lam acted creatively in his progressive interpretation of the existing constitutional "rules of the game," but always with full awareness of the contemporary practical political limits to the inherited nineteenth-century prerogative powers.

IV

—w—

FAULT-LINES

To Spend or Not To Spend

Chrétien's first two terms as prime minister (1993–1997 and 1997–2000) were dominated by fiscal issues. Indeed, the beginning of the 1990s saw a growing public awareness of an approaching financial crisis for Canada. In part, this resulted from the ever closer links to the United States economy, which was then going through its own recession. The principal cause, however, was clearly past Canadian financial policies going back over several decades, with responsibility extending not merely to the Mulroney government (1984–1993) but to the predecessor Trudeau government (1968–1979; 1980–1984). The Chrétien government, on entry into office after the October 1993 general election, inherited a $42.8 billion deficit budget for the year 1993 from the Mulroney/Campbell[62]

---

[62] Kim Campbell was PM from 25 June to 4 November 1993.

government, as well as an accumulated external national debt (including provincial debts) of more than $700 billion. The federal government's annual interest payments on its share of the external debt amounted to more than $60 billion. Together with this, and reflecting the weakness in the economy, were high inflation and high unemployment as chronic conditions of the national and provincial economies.

With a strong federal finance minister in Paul Martin, to whom the prime minister freely conceded a very large degree of autonomy and authority in the development and implementation of corrective financial measures, the dominant tone of the new government became fiscal responsibility. Cuts in the extremely high government spending were the order of the day. Indeed, so desperate was our financial situation that the International Monetary Fund and the World Bank issued public hints of international penalty listings and sanctions unless Draconian control measures were introduced by the Canadian government. There was no serious opposition to the introduction of urgent corrective measures within the government caucus or the cabinet, and public support was substantial. The announced objective of the finance minister was to achieve a balanced budget before the year 2000, and to reach this goal through successive annual budgetary cutbacks from the high-watermark of the 1993 deficit. In fact, the target of a balanced budget by the year 2000 was attained two years ahead of schedule, to be followed by a second balanced budget in 1999. This was the first such occurrence of back-to-back balanced (nodeficit) federal budgets in almost three decades.

With anticipated annual budgetary surpluses from then on — substantial budgetary surpluses that, in the event, actually surpassed the initial projections for 1999 and 2000 — a major policy dilemma arose. This was whether to utilize all or at least the most substantial portion of the expected annual budgetary surplus to amortize the huge external national debt; or whether instead to reserve a substantial portion of the new annual surplus to reduce personal income tax and corporate taxes as a means of stimulating economic growth; or whether to embark again on a generous federal spending program in areas like national health care and social services that, with rapidly rising costs in both domains, had clearly suffered materially from the financial austerity program of the mid-1990s. The initial response of the finance minister to the early achievement of his zero-deficit budget goal and to the new federal budget surpluses was to attempt to strike a balance between the restoration of Canada's external credit rating and countervailing pressures to reduce income tax and to revive the economy. One serious proposal advanced within the government caucus as to the balance that should be struck in future budgets was to allocate fifty percent of any federal surplus to income tax reductions and to the amortization of the national debt, with the other fifty percent to be reserved for "social" spending. Restoration of the financial base for the national Medicare program was advanced as the highest priority within such social spending. This was and remains a battle to be fought within the national Liberal caucus, with the lines of demarcation between the rival groups on this issue being clear enough in philosophical-ideological terms, particularly within the numerically dominant Ontario regional caucus.

Immigration and Citizenship

Immigration policies in the Chrétien era seemed to suffer from a lack of clear, overall definition of long-range government policies. Ministers like Lucienne Robillard and Elinor Caplan lacked, as newcomers to Ottawa, the seniority in the cabinet or the personal closeness to the prime minister to be able to sell any coherent national policy that they themselves might have envisioned. In consequence, immigration policies in recent years have operated with an optic of reuniting families and of giving a priority to relatives (broadly interpreted) of persons already settled in Canada. Yet, the pronounced ageing of the existing Canadian population, due to sharply falling national birth rates, meant setting a target of 270,000 immigrants per year (on the basis of one percent of the existing population at the time this unofficial quota was first set).[63] With other post-industrial societies experiencing the same ageing-population problems and the same shortage of highly skilled workers, it is not surprising that in this competition for new immigrants, Canada's unofficial annual target for regular immigrants has proved difficult to obtain, and has usually been substantially undersubscribed.

One must wonder, however, if any Canadian government has ever understood fully what it was doing in immigration matters. All other considerations aside, Canadian immigration policy from the First World War until this last decade has been largely reactive: the tap might be turned on, the tap might be turned off, depending on the rate of domestic unemployment in any given year. In 1961, for example, when unemployment was high, immigration regulations were tightened to the point that only 71,689 immigrants were admitted. In 1967, when the unemployment rate was low, 222,876 immigrants were allowed to enter. In 1978, the immigrant figure was down to 86,313; two years later it was up to 143,117. Try as they might, Canadian governments did not seem to be able to determine absorptive capacity until after the fact. More important, they were never prepared to admit their incapacity in this regard. Nor ever to admit that third-world family class immigrants and "refugees" were beginning, or, in fact, had come, to dominate Canadian immigration policy considerations to the exclusion of traditional-source European immigrants.

Canada, in the post-World War II period, has seen its population swell from 14,009,000 in 1951 to 18,238,000 in 1961, to 21,568,000 in 1971, to 24,343,000 in 1981, to 27,297,000 in 1991, to more than 30,000,000 today: an increase of more than one hundred percent in less than fifty years. That some fifteen percent of its population in 1991 had a mother tongue other than English or French, or that, as the twentieth century drew to a close, more than eighteen percent of Canadians were foreign-born, are not (historically, at least)

---

[63] Now apparently raised to a target of 300,000 per year.

remarkable statistics in themselves. What is significant is that two-thirds of the more than seven and one-half million post-World War II immigrants have been from non-traditional-source countries, including nearly two million from Asia. And that nearly a quarter-million or more immigrants arrive at our gates each year, an increasing majority of whom are from China and India.

In the years 1906–1923, 43,470 Chinese immigrated to Canada, whereas in the period 1924–1946, only seven were admitted under the racially discriminatory exclusion law of 1923. In contrast: in the years 1947–1967, this figure increased to 46,765 Chinese immigrants (not counting illegal aliens); and in the period 1967–1991, nearly 300,000 Chinese immigrants arrived from mainland China, Hong Kong, and Taiwan. In 2001, according to the decennial census, Canadians of Chinese descent[64] were the largest visible minority group, their numbers surpassing one million.

The 1971 decennial census recorded virtually no Canadians who had been born in Korea, Vietnam, Laos, or the Philippines, whereas in 1991 the figures were 33,170, 113,595, 14,445, and 123,295 respectively. These figures were in stark contrast to Canadians born in Japan, whose numbers in 1991 were only 12,280. In 1951, the census counted only 3,934 Canadians who had been born in India; in 1971, it recorded 43,645; and in 1991, 173,670 (plus 16,000 Canadians of East Indian origin born in Fiji, another 8,900 born in Uganda, and, no doubt, numbers less discernable in the census data from Kenya, Guyana, Trinidad/Tobago, Britain, etc.). The 1991 decennial census recorded 25,440 Canadians born in Sri Lanka (Ceylon); 25,180 born in Pakistan (which had been part of India until 1947); 30,715 in Iran; 12,180 in Turkey; 54,605 in Lebanon; 16,770 in Israel; as well as 85,705 born in the Middle East and other Asian countries. It is of interest (possibly even of significance) that by 1998, there were more Moslems than Jews in Canada.

---

[64] Including landed immigrants and refugee claimants from China, Hong Kong and Taiwan.

In 1971, the numbers of Canadians born in the Caribbean countries of Barbados, Guyana, Haiti, Jamaica, Trinidad-Tobago, and the smaller Island states and colonies were not statistically significant; in 1991, their combined total was nearly 300,000. The same may be noted of Canadians born in Latin America: in 1971, there were almost too few to be counted; in 1991, there were 133,925. Finally, in 1991, there were 94,615 Canadians born in sub-Saharan Africa (albeit, 24,725 of them — white, black, Indian, or "mixed," in whatever proportions — from South Africa), as well as 28,015 born in Egypt, and 16,795 in Morocco. Of the total foreign-born in Canada in 1991 (4,335,185): twenty-three percent (995,225) were from Britain, Ireland, and the United States; ten percent (447,400) from traditional-source countries in Northwestern Europe; twenty-nine percent (1,246,515) from Central, Eastern, and Southern Europe (including 161,180 who were born in Portugal); as opposed to thirty-eight percent (1,646,045) from Asia, the Caribbean, Latin America, and Africa (a percentage that has since exceeded fifty percent, and continues to rise). The top ten source countries for immigration to Canada in 1998 (in order, one to ten) were China, India, Philippines, Pakistan, Hong Kong, Taiwan, Iran, South Korea, United States, and Russia. Britain, which had been number ten in 1996 and 1997, fell off the list.

In 2001, the top ten were as follows: China (10.8 percent), India (8.5 percent), Philippines (6.7 percent), Hong Kong (6.5 percent), Sri Lanka (3.4 percent), Pakistan (3.2 percent), Taiwan (2.9 percent), United States (2.8 percent), Iran (2.6 percent), and Poland (2.4 percent). Commenting on our changing sources of immigrants, Statistics Canada, in its January 2003 release of the immigration-related figures from the 2001 census, observed, "The host of new groups includes: Kosovars from Yugoslavia; Azerbaijani and Georgians from Central Asia: Pashtun from Afghanistan; Yemeni and Saudi Arabians from the Middle East; Khmer from Southeast Asia; Nepali and Kashmiri from South Asia; Congolese, Yoruba and Ashanti from Africa; and Bolivians, Maya and Carib Indians from Central and South America." The constitutional folklore, an historically true description in 1867 (if we leave out, for the moment, the native peoples) of a country of "two founding nations," French and British, has to be balanced against the new demographic reality that we live together today in a genuinely multinational, plural-cultural Canadian society.[65]

Canada's record, and *new* reputation (as opposed to pre-World War II), as a haven for *genuine* political refugees was established long before Canada finally signed the United Nations Convention and Protocol on the Status of Refugees and Stateless Persons on 4 June 1969. It is estimated that 186,150 displaced persons of all European races and religions entered Canada in the 1947–1952 period. In 1956–58, 37,149 Hungarian refugees fleeing a brutal Soviet suppression would join them (at federal government expense for their transportation under Prime Ministers St. Laurent and Diefenbaker, but with what amounted to the "sponsorship" of the Frost and Bennett governments in Ontario and British Columbia, respectively). And 11,153 Czechs fleeing a similar Soviet terror would arrive after 1968. To which numbers we might add the 30,000 to 40,000 (or more) Americans who entered Canada in the years between 1960 and 1972 to avoid participation in the Vietnam War.

Thus, there was much precedent for Prime Minister Trudeau's acceptance (at the urging of the Aga Khan) of 7,069 Ugandan Ismailis expelled by the deranged dictator Idi Amin in 1972; 6,990 Chileans fleeing the right-wing/military coup of Augusto Pinochet after 1973; 11,010 Lebanese escaping the catastrophic consequences of civil war and foreign invasion between 1976 and 1979; and the smaller numbers of Cypriots, Kurds from Iraq, and Portuguese from Mozambique and Angola — each group fleeing their

---

[65] The electoral boundaries of my riding of Vancouver Quadra in the 1993 general election encompassed a more fully plural-cultural community than could be found in any other BC riding. Quadra, as reconfigured for purposes of the 1997 election, regrettably lost a good deal of this ethnocultural diversity. But the ties and associations with the community support groups from my original 1992–1993 party nomination campaign remained strong throughout my parliamentary tenure, and have continued since.

own particular terror. The decision of the Joe Clark government[66] to begin the process that resulted in Canada's acceptance of 113,595 Vietnamese boat people between the late 1970s and mid 1980s deserves special mention. So extraordinary was this act of national compassion that the United Nations High Commissioner for Refugees presented the people of Canada with the 1986 Nansen Medal for their service to the refugee cause.

Some highly contentious elements, however, remain in Canada's new immigration policies and practice. First, it has been difficult to control and to regulate the flood of persons who arrive in Canada, outside regular immigration rules and procedures, and who then immediately claim refugee status. Once in Canada, even though illegally arrived, a person who then claims refugee status, cannot be deported under Canadian law, except at the conclusion of a very lengthy and cumbersome administrative review process that lasts a minimum of three years — and that may be prolonged indefinitely (for a decade, or more) by resourceful lawyers who know how to exhaust appellate judicial review. This has brought a few spectacular cases of well-financed international drug cartel members, crime syndicate leaders, and felons convicted of heinous crimes who have been able successfully to defy all attempts by the government to deport them in timely fashion.

Mixed up with clearly genuine refugee claimant cases, such well-publicized instances of apparent abuse of Canadian law and legal processes have created unnecessary political barriers to an even more generous, open door policy on refugees. Among those objecting to alleged abuses in the refugee admissions program have been members of new cultural communities, themselves originally immigrants, who point out that they came to Canada in full conformity to the letter and also the spirit of Canadian law, and had put up, cheerfully, with long delays in those regular immigration processes. Unfortunately, ministerial plans in recent years for

---

[66] And in particular, Clark's minister of employment and immigration, Ron Atkey.

amendment of the national immigration laws to close such loopholes generally seem to have been curtailed or dropped because of
difficulties of reaching a clear consensus within the government
and, even more, within the government caucus (and its Ontario
wing in particular).

A remaining immigration policy dilemma — and it is really a
post-immigration issue — goes to the question of the status of immigrants once they are successfully "received" into the general community. For the last decade or so, citizenship and immigration
have been joined once more in the same portfolio.[67] A decision on
citizenship policy has inevitable consequences for immigration
policies. The early citizenship policy of the Trudeau government
was one announced as multiculturalism — a rather vague and
open-ended concept usually manifested politically (governmental-
ly) through the organization of symbolic immigrant folk festivals
and similar public entertainments. A potentially subtler policy approach was summed up in the idea of Canada as a "community of
communities" — embraced by Joe Clark during his short prime
ministership. This was a concept developed by the philosopher
Martin Buber, who was born as a citizen of the multiracial Austro-
Hungarian empire, but who eventually emigrated to Israel.[68] Rein-
terpreted in a contemporary context, its significance would appear
to be in its conscious differentiation not only from the American
"melting-pot" idea of a total absorption of new immigrant groups
and the synthesis of their cultures into a common national culture,
but also from the pre-1914 continental European model of separate national, ethnocultural communities represented separately

---

[67] As opposed to manpower and immigration or employment and immigration — portfolio unions that began under Pearson and continued under
Trudeau, Clark, Mulroney, and into Chrétien's first term.

[68] Buber had projected the new, postwar state of Israel as an ideal testing-
ground for his ideas, based on late nineteenth- and early twentieth-century
Habsburg empire practice of a tolerant pluralism on minority cultural-
linguistic issues. Buber's concept and his special terminology — "community
of communities" — apparently came to Prime Minister Clark through PMO
research staff.

in the national legislature and other public forums. In Canada, immigrant communities have been encouraged to maintain a distinct and separate cultural development, while entering into the political process on the same equal basis as everyone else.

In the end, an urgent reexamination of immigration and refugee policies by the federal government may have been accelerated by the 11 September 2001 terrorist actions in New York City, and resulting pressures by the United States administration for a common North American "security perimeter." The coordination of basic Canadian and American immigration and refugee policy appears a condition of maintaining the "open frontier" between the two countries and the relatively unhindered "free passage" of goods and people across those boundaries. Travel warnings by the Canadian foreign ministry — a full thirteen months after the 11 September terrorist incident — to Canadian citizens of Iranian, Iraqi, Libyan, Sudanese and Syrian origin to be wary about entering the United States were realistic. Indeed, Canadian passportholders in these particular categories were now subject to special US border control measures of scrutiny, including being photographed, fingerprinted and, in certain cases, questioned at length. It was later announced that landed immigrants in Canada of certain mainly Asian and African origins would have to obtain visas to enter the United States as visitors, necessitating considerable advance application and special fees.

A Canadian citizen holding dual citizenship — in the event, having retained his original Syrian nationality — was arrested in New York and deported to Syria for interrogations there.[69] In the present situation, any resulting irritations for new Canadian citizens or Canadian citizens of dual nationality might best be overcome by Ottawa moving with greater dispatch to coordinate Canadian security criteria and procedures more closely with those of the United

---

[69] These cases simply reflect the elemental principle of international law that each state may set its own standards and conditions for allowing entry into its territories by foreign nationals; that dual or multiple citizenship allows any one of the states of nationality to opt to ask for deportation to their territories.

States. In the meantime, Canadian ministers and officials — in the foreign affairs and immigration departments in particular — would appear to have some special obligation to explain the situation to categories of Canadian citizens and landed immigrants affected by the new US rules, and the new post-"9-11" political reality in the United States.

Aboriginal Affairs

The geographical fault lines in Canadian federalism today are accentuated by the political engagement of the federal government and the government of British Columbia in proceeding to the conclusion of intergovernmental agreements (treaties) resolving contested native land issues. Although such native land treaties had been part of the political-legal landscape in the rest of Canada for periods of up to a century and more, only one such treaty has been concluded so far in BC: the treaty with the Nisga'a people of the Nass River valley.[70] Initialed by both the federal and provincial governments and by the Nisga'a administration on 4 August 1998, it came into effect on 11 May 2000. The Nisga'a treaty remains fiercely contested politically within BC, however. The provincial Liberal government elected in early 2001 had pledged to challenge its constitutionality before the courts, and had promised a province-wide referendum on the principles to govern any future treaties that might be entered into by the province as part of the three-way negotiating process of federal government, provincial government, and Indian nations. While the legal challenge was quickly dropped by the new government after its election, the referendum promise remained, fueling criticism from federal quarters and, far more strongly, from BC native leaders. In the end, the new government took most of the political teeth out of the referendum

---

[70] Again, this is to ignore, for practical purposes, the handful of treaties signed by Governor James Douglas on Vancouver Island before Confederation with Canada in 1871, and the extension of Treaty No. 8 into northeastern BC during the Klondike gold rush in 1899.

proposal, reducing it to a mail-in vote with largely trite and innocu-
ous questions. Political confrontation was avoided, but at the apparent price of further delays in the treaty-negotiation process.

The problem of negotiation of new native land claims, or revision and updating of old claims, is made more complex in BC, in
comparison to the other provinces, by the absence of any substantial and continuing experience, on the part of both native and
non-native communities in the political give-and-take necessary for
achieving contemporary consensual solutions. This has led to a
certain absolutism on the part of aboriginal leaders in the pre-
senting of land claims, as well as some rhetorical exaggeration in
their formulation. The relevant legal briefs and public statements
in support seem most often to be prepared and presented by non-
native lawyers, and this may account for some of the verbal excesses. Thus, for example, with some fifty-odd native land treaties
actually being negotiated, or still to be negotiated in British Columbia, it has been estimated that the various native land claims,
in their totality, might amount to well over one hundred percent
of the total land surface of the province. The main burden of the
legal costs and of the legal fees of the lawyers involved is borne
today by the federal government, and thus by all Canadian tax-
payers. In the past, the legal work was usually done by academic
lawyers charging only nominal expenses, or by private lawyers acting *pro bono publico*.

There is a wealth of difference between some of the current
demands in BC and earlier formulations of aboriginal rights that
were advanced by the Cree Nations (Treaty Nations Nos. 6, 7, and
8 of Alberta and Saskatchewan, and Treaty Nation No. 9 of Ontario) a full two decades ago in the lead-up to Trudeau's 1980–1982
constitutional patriation project. To establish their well-reasoned
case for aboriginal self-government within the Canadian constitution, the Cree nations correctly mounted an assault on the classical international law premise on which, historically, the rival English and French colonial claims to sovereign title to present-day
Canada had been based. This was the concept of *res nullius*. That is
to say, that it was territory unoccupied by "civilized nations" and

therefore open to assertion of sovereignty by any European power arriving in the territory and manifesting and then maintaining an intention to that effect. It was an important political-legal step for native leaders to challenge the *res nullius* concept as applied to Canada, although the Cree Nations leaders did not themselves innovate, but followed on the international law expositions made by the International Court of Justice in 1975 in a celebrated ruling in the *Western Sahara* case on vestigial Spanish Colonial territories and the rights in them of indigenous native peoples.[71]

In the *Western Sahara* case, the International Court had recognized the relativism, in space-time terms, of the West European-derived notion of fixed territorial frontiers, and had indicated that wise contemporary solutions required balancing that notion with moving frontier practices and customs of other and earlier (non-European) nomadic societies in the African territories impacted by European colonialism. The rational conclusion, in case of conflict between competing cultures with regard to their respective claims, would require a certain respect for subsequently acquired rights, vested over a period of years and then a striking of some sort of equitable weighting between them and original, aboriginal claims to title. This is a process that usually lends itself better to arbitral settlement than to adjudication. Leaving the decision on such rival claims to the often highly artificial requirements of court rulings usually results in one side winning absolutely and the other side losing absolutely. However, on equitable grounds, all the competing claims would suggest themselves as deserving of some degree of acceptance and legal recognition.

The Supreme Court of Canada, in some recent jurisprudence,

---

[71] It is one thing to challenge legal doctrines formulated in an earlier, Eurocentrist era of international law, but quite a large jump from that to argue that all subsequent historical developments and the acquired rights flowing from them can thereby be ignored. The history of the world community is one of constant movement of peoples across vast territories. The notion of fixed, immutable territorial frontiers is one peculiar, in space-time terms, to the period following on the Peace of Westphalia in 1648, with the emergence of the "modern" period in international relations and the new European states founded on the rise of commerce.

the formulations of which strayed a little beyond the legal necessities of the case and perhaps also the bounds of political prudence, seemed to indicate that in aboriginal rights claims ordinary rules of evidentiary proof could be down-weighted, with oral evidence, only loosely defined, accepted in its place. While the seeming absolutism of such early judicial dicta appears to have been corrected by the Supreme Court in its later jurisprudence and rulings on what types of proof will be accepted, general public reading of the original rulings may have contributed to current political difficulties in the treaty-making process, thus often encouraging the respective parties to take rigid, no-compromise positions in their mutual negotiations.

The federal government has hardly helped the courts or other parties to the treaty negotiating process by a continuing failure to provide leadership in charting out macro-policy positions. The Cree Nations first formulated their concept of an "inherent right to self-government," when I was their *ad hoc* constitutional adviser during the Trudeau "patriation" round. It was not to chart out any bid to self-determination and autonomy *outside* the Canadian constitutional system, but simply to reaffirm, in a Canadian context, Rousseau's central idea from the eighteenth-century age of Enlightenment that the right to govern oneself comes, not as a gift of any government or governments, but from one's inherent capacity as a human being. This argument was employed during the Trudeau round in 1980–1982 to argue for the recognition of a constitutional status, still to be refined and concretized as to its modalities, within the existing Canadian federal system and subject at all times to the Canadian constitution.

Prime Minister Trudeau and, later and separately, the then governor general, Edward Schreyer, had direct personal meetings with the Cree leaders at that time. The native constitutional arguments (as well as the way in which they were presented) seemed reasonable and capable of leading to pragmatic constitutional accommodations. However, disagreement with the national Indian leadership (and within the Cree Nations), plus rapid changes on the federal-provincial constitutional battlefront, meant that the Cree proposals as to the "inherent right of self-government" lapsed politically at the time. These proposals were revived again during the Meech Lake and Charlottetown extended constitutional debate, but their *raison d'être* as a negotiating point of departure toward pragmatic accommodation within the existing federal system by then had been largely forgotten, both within Ottawa's ministry of Indian affairs and within the larger national First Nations leadership. This was a pity, because the proposals, taken out of their original context, became misunderstood and then distorted into a form of confrontation and claim for some *extra-constitutional* status, or even separation from Canada for the Indian nations.

Similar confusions and cloudy thinking seem to have attended recent federal ministry reactions to threats of collective, class-action suits by aboriginal former students against the main Christian churches in Canada. The churches, at the behest of the national governments in earlier periods, had undertaken the task of educating aboriginal children in much of Northern and Western Canada. That some number of the children involved had been abused by their teachers was admitted. And where criminal misconduct by teachers was clear, it would be prosecuted under the criminal law. What was not in any way established was that the education so provided was not generally of a high professional standard, or that there was widespread and systematic abuse of the children by their teachers.

Experience with class-action suits of this general character in the United States, directed by private lawyers operating on a contingent fee basis, suggests the relative ease with which suits can proliferate with respect to events alleged to have occurred many years before and not protested publicly at the time or in the intervening years since that time. Ottawa may have been too slow to acknowledge the sheer dimension of the problem, or the federal government's own share in any delictual responsibility, if this should later be demonstrated by accepted standards of legal proof to have come into play. Having delegated its own constitutional responsibility, in the first place, to private religious organizations, Ottawa nevertheless retained, at all times, a duty-of-care relationship with the parties to monitor the delegated activities and to intervene actively in any resulting law suits and to acknowledge the government's own shared financial responsibility. The federal government's interventions, such as these were, came very late and only after the churches had raised, publicly, the issue of the enormous daily burden of litigation costs that they were having to assume because of the welter of latter-day law suits launched against them.

Prime Minister Chrétien, after the matter was raised in the national caucus, asked his longest serving colleague, the then deputy prime minister, Herb Gray, to take over the file. Gray's response, eighteen months later, was a proposal that the government offer to pay seventy percent of the total amount of the claims involved, with the churches to assume the remaining thirty percent. Gray had joined issue with the churches' contention that the system of church-administered education in the North and West was a federal government response to the problem of aboriginal education. The churches had contended that their own involvement was entirely secondary, with the churches having entered into aboriginal education only reluctantly and at Ottawa's insistence, because no other solution was available.

The federal government, however, did not canvas a central and most troubling legal aspect of the latter-day class suits. That is to say, their emergence long after the alleged events, when difficulties of proving claims and establishing their credibility must become extreme. A recent report by one of Canada's most respected jurists, retired Quebec Court of Appeal Justice Fred Kaufman, into the government of Nova Scotia response in 1995 to allegations of abuse in provincial youth institutions, had highlighted the problem of credibility and proof of legal claims from a long-distant past. Justice Kaufman noted that the original eighty-nine cases of alleged youth abuse had suddenly swelled with press publicity to 1,264. The provincial government had then paid out $30 million to alleged victims, without any testing, by normal evidentiary rules, of events supposedly occurring twenty to forty years earlier, and never before reported. A similar amount of money apparently went to the lawyers involved in the cases for their professional legal fees.

On another issue, this time within my own constituency of Vancouver Quadra, I had concluded that a long-festering and very public dispute over the renewal of the Musqueam leaseholds had not been helped by the ministry of Indian affairs' hands-off attitude. This had broken out into the open with recent massive increases in the leasehold rentals (more than doubled in most cases) imposed by the Musqueam Band on the predominantly non-aboriginal leaseholders. In addition, there was the menace of a hostile federal government intervention against these leaseholders in pending litigation against them launched by the Musqueam Band.

The leaseholds had originally been created by the federal government directly, through individual contracts between the federal government and the non-aboriginal leaseholders. But then, without any prior consultation or advice to the leaseholders, the Trudeau government had unilaterally transferred the leaseholds to the legal control of the Musqueam band. A later federal government (the Mulroney Conservatives) had subsequently unilaterally transferred the power to tax the leaseholds to the Musqueam Band — again without any prior consultation or advice to the leaseholders. Such ministry conduct would seem to be less than might be expected from the federal government in its contractual relations with its citizens.

Under pressure to answer, ministry spokespersons declared that the ministry was legally constrained now to act as "trustee" for the Indian bands only, and could not consider other, non-aboriginal interests. While this "trustee" analogy might be true in a high symbolic sense (if not in the generally understood strict legal sense), it remained a fact that the government of Canada and its ministers — indeed, like every MP — are trustee in the same large sense for all the people of Canada, aboriginals and non-aboriginals alike. The obligation is to render equity to all. Failure by the federal ministry to at least acknowledge this larger, *inclusive* community legal responsibility helped produce some of the evident public uneasiness or hostility in British Columbia as to what Ottawa viewed as its own special constitutional role and mission in the ongoing native land treaty negotiating process in BC. It may also have contributed to the long delays and also the political opposition in BC to the Nisga'a Treaty.

As earlier indicated, I had no problems at all with the Nisga'a Treaty. The Nisga'a leader, Chief Joe Gosnell, was firmly polite, patient and softly-spoken at all times. He was highly pragmatic in his give-and-take approach to the federal and provincial government representatives. He accepted, willingly, additions that I and others had proposed that made the Nisga'a Treaty subject to the constitution of Canada and to the Canadian Charter of Rights and Freedoms. This was necessary in our view to reassure local (non-aboriginal) BC citizens that the Nisga'a Treaty, in its concrete application and administration, would always remain subject to Charter-based principles of due process of law and administrative fairness; and that the Nisga'a Treaty would be controllable, as such, by the ordinary courts of the land in case of need. Jane Stewart's successor as Indian affairs minister, Bob Nault, after a difficult learning process with the Musqueam leaseholders, announced in June 2002, a large-scale reform of the Indian Act, largely untouched since then Indian affairs minister Chrétien's disappointed attempts three decades before.[72] Proposed reforms included enforcing democratic voting rights in band elections; public accountability of band leaders for their expenditure of the huge federal grants; and general application of the Charter or Rights to internal band affairs. There was some support for this from band rank-and-file, and particularly female members, but entrenched band chieftains have vowed a fierce resistance to any change.

---

[72] Jean Chrétien was minister of Indian affairs and northern development from 6 July 1968 to 8 August 1974. His ill-fated policy paper (a "white paper" by any other name), which advocated phasing out the department of Indian affairs and transferring services for Native Canadians to the provinces, was tabled in the House of Commons in June 1969.

Quebec Fact and Western "Alienation"

The near-miss failure of the Meech Lake Accord, and then the spectacular rejection of the Charlottetown Agreement in the nationwide popular referendum of 1992, ended the attempts by the Mulroney government to bring to a successful conclusion any attempt by English-Canada to respond to the constitutional imperatives of Quebec's quiet revolution. This double constitutional defeat was all the more frustrating for the Mulroney government because it had attempted to rally support from the English-speaking provinces by advancing significant reform for the constitution as a whole, including modernization of two of the more controversial federal institutions in political terms, the nonelected Senate and the Supreme Court of Canada. Mulroney had succeeded in persuading the Quebec government to modify some of its original negotiating demands for constitutional recognition and entrenchment of the "French fact" in Quebec. The Bourassa government in Quebec had yielded to Mulroney's advice on this point, as being a politically necessary concession to the English-speaking provinces.

A principal lesson drawn from this double failure of constitutional reform under the Mulroney government was that, after the initial public interest and excitement engendered by the Trudeau constitutional project, the general public had become tired, and eventually bored with the seemingly endless constitutional debate that appeared more and more to be addressed to, and carried on by, the highly remunerated "cottage industry" of lawyers and professors and consultants who had grown prosperous feeding on the constitution. There were, of course, other not inconsiderable factors explaining the defeats of Meech Lake and Charlottetown. One was a rapidly diminishing popularity of the sponsoring Mulroney government toward the end of the two successive, large majority governments. Another was the seemingly visceral grass-roots reaction in English-speaking Canada against what was viewed as an excessive preoccupation or fixation by Ottawa with the "French fact," and with Quebec's special constitutional demands.[73]

Whatever the final conclusion as to why the Canadian public voted NO on the Charlottetown Accord in 1992, there was no real doubt as to the conclusion drawn by national party strategists who planned the succeeding successful general election campaign that yielded the majority Liberal government in October 1993. As soon as the federal election had been won, Jean Chrétien proceeded to close the constitutional files. He thus liberated his new ministry from the sort of special high-profile cabinet charge that had emerged when the constitutional debate was at its height in the 1970s and 1980s.[74] Such constitutional issues as might arise could if necessary always be dealt with, *ad hoc*, by the new Justice Minister Allan Rock, a very able civil litigator, but not a constitutional lawyer. Except for Prime Minister Chrétien himself, there was no one with claims to constitutional expertise in the new government. Where had all the articulate constitutionalists who had graced the front rows of the government and the opposition in the House of Commons in the Trudeau and Mulroney years disappeared to?

It was understandable enough for Chrétien to make fiscal responsibility the prime goal of his new government and to give it priority over everything else. The argument may be made, however, that it was not in conflict with these particular fiscal priorities to venture, at the same time, into new policy-making on other, non-fiscal fronts. What emerged, in fact, was a government policy of *attente,* or waiting, on other major policy issues, and above all on issues of reform and modernization of the federal system and the constitution of 1867 (Quebec issues and non-Quebec issues alike).

---

[73] The latter point was certainly reinforced in the popular referendum debate in 1992 by a perception that excessive concessions had been made to Quebec that were patently unreasonable in relation to the rest of the country. A particularly controversial example cited was the constitutional guarantee to Quebec under the Charlottetown Agreement of twenty-five percent of the seats in the House of Commons in perpetuity, and this notwithstanding any future changes in Quebec's percentage of the total population of the country.

[74] The most notable example is the constitutional affairs portfolio, as entrusted by Prime Minister Mulroney to former prime minister Joe Clark.

There was certainly no public criticism of this politic of constitutional *laissez-faire*, and no excitement at all within Parliament or demand from the opposition side for new constitutional action.

Acting on his own initiative on the opposition side, the Reform party's then constitutional critic, Stephen Harper, had several times raised questions in the House over the wisest approach to any future Quebec referendum on "sovereignty-association," or on Quebec separation from Canada generally. Harper had picked up some constitutional advice I had offered to then Prime Minister Trudeau, before the first such referendum in 1980, and which I had republished in an op- ed page essay in *Le Devoir* in 1994.[75] I had contended that the federal government, having plenary constitutional powers in that domain, was not legally obligated to allow a provincial referendum on secession. In my opinion, Ottawa conserved the full legal options either legally to block Quebec's referendum legislation, or even to preempt Quebec's referendum by organizing its own referendum on the same question within the province of Quebec alone, or nationwide. Furthermore, I had suggested that, on a strictly legal basis, the federal government had the constitutional authority to move in the Supreme Court of Canada to "correct" any provincial referendum question so as to ensure that it would be an "honest" question (i.e., clear and unambiguous).

In my communications to Prime Minister Trudeau in the run-up to the 1980 referendum, I had made clear that these were strictly *legal* opinions. I understood that it would be a matter of high political judgement for the federal government as to whether to exercise its constitutional-legal options in this way, or whether, instead, to bite the bullet politically and to go in and fight any Quebec referendum. This is, of course, what Trudeau without hesitation opted to do. And he won triumphantly by a twenty percent-plus

---

[75] I had further revisited these discussions, and my legal opinion and political recommendation based thereon, in English, in an article in the *Canadian Parliamentary Review* in the Autumn of 1994.

margin, including, it was reliably calculated, a majority of the francophone vote.

However, when the opposition MP for Calgary West directly cited these opinions in question period on 17 October 1994, and asked if they reflected the constitutional position of the government of Canada, Marcel Massé, then minister of intergovernmental affairs, chose not to respond on the substantive issues, saying, instead, that it was a "hypothetical question." This was, of course, a year before the second Quebec referendum vote took place. On 13 May 1996, six months after this vote with its hairline majority rejecting the "sovereignty-association" proposal, Harper repeated the identical question in question period. This time, Justice Minister Allan Rock spoke for the government. Instead of answering Harper's question, he took the opportunity of responding to constitutional positions taken by the Quebec attorney-general in some recent litigation in which Ottawa had intervened. Rock then recorded the "direct and substantial opposition" of the federal government to the notion (which he attributed to the Quebec attorney general) that any future Quebec "sovereignty-association" referendum "if it results in a positive vote, can supplant or replace the constitution and the rule of law so that they have no application to the consequences."

So far as the 1995 Quebec referendum is concerned, the Chrétien government underestimated the continuing level of political dissatisfaction among Quebec's francophone majority with the state of the Canadian federal system, and Quebec's role therein. The federal government had not done any new work on the constitutional files since its election in October 1993, and it had no new proposals to offer Quebec voters. Perhaps because of an overestimation of its own popularity in the polls, the Chrétien government avoided (just as Trudeau had done before 1980) the quite considerable range of legal options available to control or limit any intentionally mischievous or colourable action by the Quebec government in establishing the timing and modalities of Quebec's approach to any further "sovereignty-association" referendum. The significant difference was that Trudeau had possessed the confidence and the *élan* (and a highly effective ministerial team including then federal justice minister Jean Chrétien) to go into the provincial referendum battle and win, elegantly and decisively. He took up the challenge politically and responded politically.

With the second Quebec referendum a decade and a half later, it was not really until the last week of the campaign, when Chrétien's advance public opinion polling results for Quebec were in, that the possibility of a debacle for the federal forces emerged. It was then that the alarm buttons were pressed in Ottawa. A last-minute drive spearheaded by the prime minister and then federal fisheries minister Brian Tobin brought a massive federal intervention, which may perhaps have snatched victory from the jaws of defeat on an intentionally "soft" and ambiguous (and potentially constitutionally-legally vulnerable) Quebec government question. In the final tally, a mere 50.6 percent of Quebec voters opted to stay in Canada.

After his government's narrow escape in the second Quebec referendum, Chrétien decided to reopen the constitutional files. But this was on a narrow, Quebec-oriented basis only, avoiding the larger issues of general institutional reform and modernization that might bring in support from all regions, and not be restricted to Quebec. The prime minister chose as his *porte-parole* in the House of Commons on Quebec issues, and as a new minister of intergovernmental affairs, a politically unknown academic from Montreal without professional-academic formation and specialization or prior direct political experience in constitutional law or on federal questions. Stéphane Dion performed bravely enough in the House, but with the government itself vacillating between a hard line and a softer, somewhat more conciliatory approach toward Quebec nationalism — what was labeled, euphemistically, as Plan A and Plan B — Dion's assigned role as minister was to be the one to say NO! In the result, the exchanges in the House between the new minister and the opposition *Bloc Québécois* became something of a dialogue of the deaf, with unbroken monologues delivered at breakneck speed — to enthusiastic applause from the one side, and mocking, derisive laughter from the other. As had happened after the first independence referendum in 1980, the high fever of the campaign for public support was followed in both Quebec and in Canada as a whole by a period of weariness and boredom. Constitutional esoterica were passed up for more mundane and immediate, financial and economic priorities. Would we now be given another decade and a half of relative calm on the Quebec constitutional front, as had happened after the vote in 1980?

Chrétien did use the post-referendum reactive calm to introduce, as a joint resolution of both Houses of Parliament, a formal recognition of Quebec as a "distinct society" within the Canadian confederation, as well as according to Quebec a veto over future projects for federal constitutional change. He had promised this to Quebec voters in the dying days of the 1995 referendum campaign, and it may perhaps have contributed positively to the hairline federal majority in the actual vote. A joint parliamentary resolution, however, did not qualify as an entrenched constitutional amendment. There would be nothing, in strictly legal terms, to prevent either the Commons or the Senate from departing from it in the future. But as a matter of the politics of the constitution, there was some general acceptance of the persuasive authority of Chrétien's gesture, particularly since the text of the resolution, as adopted in December 1995, had been widened to include a right of veto for other "regions" of Canada in addition to Quebec.

The new continentalism, discussed below, resulting from the world-wide trends towards trans-national economic association and coordination of key decision-making on common problems that transcend conventional national frontiers, contributes to a general perception that sovereignty is an increasingly dated concept that stands in the way of the new political and economic realities. On some views, the separatist cause in Quebec may have peaked at the time of the October, 1995 sovereignty-association referendum and is now becoming a declining force because of demographic changes in Quebec resulting from falling natality rates and the new immigrant waves from non-traditional sources.

In the Quebec provincial elections of 14 April 2003, the separatist *Parti Québécois* government, after nine years in office, was replaced by a majority Quebec Liberal Party government led by former Mulroney Conservative government minister and Deputy Prime Minister in the short-lived Kim Campbell Conservative government of 1993, Jean Charest. If Charest, as expected, should try to make common cause, in federal-provincial relations, with provincial leaders from other provinces, we might see a return to the vibrant, cooperative federalism demanded in the 1960s by provincial leaders like Lesage, Robarts, Manning and W.A.C. Bennett and encouraged, at the federal level, by Prime Minister Lester Pearson.

In particular, following on interventions by MPs and Senators in the national caucus and elsewhere in public, the government had extended its original concept of a veto for four traditional "regions" of Canada — Quebec, Ontario, the Atlantic provinces, and the West — so as to include British Columbia as a "region" in its own right. This was longtime BC Social Credit Premier W.A.C. Bennett's conception of his province as a *fifth* region of Canada, coequal constitutionally with the other regions — something he had first enunciated at the "Confederation of Tomorrow" provincial premiers conference, hosted and chaired by Ontario Premier John Robarts in 1967. At last, Bennett's dream had found *de facto* realization in federal legislative terms, if not yet entrenchment in the constitution.[76]

Was Prime Minister Chrétien too pessimistic in his reading of the lessons from the Mulroney government's Meech Lake and Charlottetown failures, as to the capacity and willingness of the Canadian public to consider and accept proposals for fundamental change in the federal system of government going beyond purely Quebec issues? Or did he simply fear anything that would divert the intellectual energy and enthusiasm of Canadians from his

---

[76] One should mention that after the failure of the Liberal party to make electoral progress in British Columbia in 1997, a special Western desk was added in the PMO, staffed by a knowledgeable Westerner, Pam McDonald.

government's priorities of the time, predominantly fiscal as these were? I think it was a little of both. In the result, the ageing of the Westminster-style institutions "received" from imperial Britain in 1867 continued, with all the evident problems in the attrition of the parliamentary processes and their failure to be adapted to contemporary community problems and problem-solving.

In terms of federal-provincial relations, what was widely viewed as an overly preemptive concern with Quebec demands to the exclusion of other regional complaints, brought continuing dissension over Ottawa's cutbacks in its financial transfer programs to the provinces. These cutbacks, in the provinces' views, had seriously undermined their ability to deliver on health and education and related social programs which fell within their spheres of exclusive legal competence under the constitution. Some of the frictions in federal-provincial relations of the period now took on the character of outright guerilla warfare. For example, when Ottawa seemed unable to resolve an ongoing dispute over US overfishing of Pacific coast salmon stocks, the NDP government of British Columbia under its bright young premier, Glen Clark, threatened to close down the underwater testing range used by the United States Navy to test unarmed nuclear missiles. The federal government retaliated by expropriating the territory involved.

The change in government in British Columbia in May 2001 brought in a Liberal government with a new premier, Gordon Campbell. In his public statements during the provincial election campaign, Campbell had indicated a desire to establish close political relations with other provinces (including Quebec). This could eventually presage, if there were to be an obdurate centralist approach maintained in Ottawa, a provincial coalition of forces of the sort experienced in the 1960s by the Diefenbaker and Pearson governments when strong provincial premiers — Jean Lesage and Daniel Johnson in Quebec, John Robarts in Ontario, Ernest Manning in Alberta, and W.A.C. Bennett in British Columbia — made common cause in demanding that Ottawa initiate concrete measures in federal-provincial intergovernmental cooperation.

The contemporary parallel may emerge from Chrétien's decision to have the federal government ratify the so-called Kyoto Accords, the product of a long-negotiated diplomatic consensus creating new international and national norms and standards on climate and controls on emission of noxious gases by industrialized countries. The United States, of course, has indicated that it will not accept or implement Kyoto, which leaves several key provincial premiers — Klein in Alberta, Eves in Ontario, and Campbell in British Columbia — with a political dilemma. As they apparently still see this, Canada's decision to implement the Accords will result in massive shutdowns in industries within their provinces and losses of employment because of the extra burdens thrown on them in comparison to their competitors in the United States. In their view, there also will be a large incentive for some industries to relocate from their provinces. Since, in Canadian constitutional terms, much, if not most, of the substance of implementation of the Kyoto Accords in legislative form in Canada falls within lawmaking competences of the provinces, there will be considerable pressures on the provincial governments that feel themselves prejudiced by the accords to sit on their hands and to refuse to implement them.

Ottawa, of course, always could attempt a legal riposte by going to the Supreme Court to seek an overruling of the 1937 *Labour Conventions* ruling of the Judicial Committee of the Privy Council,[77] which effectively places so much of the implementation of the Kyoto Accords within lawmaking competences of the provinces. Such an overruling might have been possible in the 1950s and 1960s when this decision was being critically reexamined by jurists

---

[77] Under a celebrated ruling in 1937 of the Judicial Committee of the Privy Council, in the *Labour Conventions* case, it was decided that while the federal government had the sole and exclusive constitutional power to make treaties on behalf of Canada, that is, to sign and ratify the treaties, the concrete *implementation* of such treaties in Canadian internal law would turn on whether the necessary legislative power to do that was either federal or provincial under sections 91 and 92 of the Constitution Act of 1867, or possibly both federal and provincial.

(including its main judicial author Lord Wright) in both Britain and Canada. It would be less likely today, however, in view of a more general acceptance of the good sense of the 1937 ruling's rationale. Kyoto was just the sort of federal-provincial intergovernmental stand-off that the Pearson conception of cooperative federalism had been designed to prevent and cure. The fault today, if any, on the federal side must be placed at the door of the ministry of intergovernmental affairs which, with a preemptive concern for the theoretical abstractions of Quebec sovereignty-association, had passed over the dynamic, "living law" of give and take and cooperation between Ottawa and the provinces in concrete cases where the reciprocity and mutual benefit were clear and obvious enough.[78]

The New Continentalism

The folklore of Canadian foreign policy — increasingly difficult to live up to in a world community that is now near universal in its effective state membership — goes back to the immediate post-World War II years when the British Commonwealth (the erstwhile British empire) had become an un-prefixed Commonwealth of Nations, but when the postwar "winds of change" and the wave of decolonization and independence had yet to move beyond the Indian subcontinent. Canada, with a small cadre of cultivated, classically trained and usually British-educated diplomats, and itself free from too much wartime dislocation and so experiencing a remarkable economic growth, was in a position to provide new ideas and new approaches to international relations in place of the old European balance-of-power concepts. Under Mike Pearson[79]

---

[78] It may be that Prime Minister Chrétien, in relieving David Anderson of his responsibilities as political minister for BC, actually did Anderson (and Canada) a considerable service. Anderson is the first federal environment minister in many years to be considered a specialist in the field and really comfortable with the problem solving involved. He thus is free to devote all his energies to the urgent new problems post-Kyoto.

[79] First as foreign minister (secretary of state for external affairs) in the St. Laurent government, 1948–1957, and then as prime minister, 1963–1968.

and his able and erudite ministerial colleague Paul Martin, Sr.,[80] Canada was able to assume intellectual leadership within the Commonwealth, as well as providing leading-edge ideas at the United Nations and in the Western political-military alliance system.

It was Pearson who, as foreign minister, developed the concept of a United Nations peace-keeping force, interposed between contending parties in a conflict, each of whom might, at a certain moment in time, be ready to retreat if this could be done without intolerable loss of face. The first such United Nations Emergency Force (UNEF) was devised to meet the Suez crisis of 1956, and it gained strength from Pearson's keen understanding of the psychological elements in leadership. Pearson's plan enabled the British and French to withdraw with as much grace and dignity as possible from their joint military action together with Israel, against Egypt's Colonel Nasser, after Nasser had nationalized the British-French owned Suez Canal Company. The British-French military intervention had proceeded more slowly than anticipated, and the US secretary of state, John Foster Dulles, had threatened withdrawal of US dollar support for the British pound sterling and the French franc if they did not end their neocolonialist adventure. Pearson's plan facilitated the British-French retreat.[81] It was under Canada's Conservative government from 1957 to 1963 that Prime Minister John Diefenbaker and his foreign minister, Howard Green, took the initiative within the Commonwealth to force the withdrawal (in reality, expulsion) of the white minority-ruled Union of South Africa, in a general Commonwealth protest against its *apartheid* racial exclusion legislation and practice.

---

[80] As health minister with a supporting role at the United Nations, and then as Pearson's foreign minister.

[81] The importance of Pearson's efforts found appropriate recognition when he was awarded the Nobel Peace Prize in 1957. Unfortunately, this high achievement appears to have served as a siren song for his successors as foreign minister (and even more for their political staffers). Certainly, in recent years, Canadian foreign ministers have seemed too often tempted to overstep the limits of the politically possible, and to engage in rhetorical excesses beyond their capacity prudently to deliver.

There was a natural philosophical affinity between the Canadian political leaders of this early postwar period and post-decolonization and independence intellectual liberals like Nehru and his mercurial foreign minister, Krishna Menon, in India. Close cooperation with India's new government and similar leaders in other emerging countries inside the United Nations and in other international arenas became a cornerstone of Canadian foreign policy in what, in retrospect, now appears as its golden era, where reason and the logic of history were consciously applied in the progressive development of international law. Within the United Nations, Canada had warmly supported the celebrated uniting-for-peace resolution, adopted by the UN general assembly in late 1950 by near unanimity, which affirmed that if the UN security council should become blocked because of the exercise of a big power veto, in the undertaking of its primary responsibility for the maintenance of international peace and security, then the general assembly might move of its own accord (necessarily by a two-thirds majority vote on an "important" question) to take its own affirmative measures to maintain peace. Five years later, Paul Martin, Sr. was the principal architect within the United Nations in negotiating the famous "package deal" compromise between the Western and Soviet blocs, at the height of the Cold War, which ended the paralysis in admission of new states to the United Nations caused by each bloc's insisting on vetoing candidates for admission proposed by the other side. The principle of a necessary representative, universal character to the United Nations and its membership, in spite of ideological differences, was thus accepted and has been observed, almost without exception, since that time, as a result of Paul Martin, Sr.'s deadlock-breaking, pragmatic initiative.

With the progressive unfolding and completion of the historical processes of decolonization and independence and the downfall of European imperialism, the initial leadership role that Canada had with the "small" United Nations immediately following on its creation in 1945 was bound to decline. Starting off with fifty-one members in 1945 and jumping (with Paul Martin, Sr.'s "package deal") from sixty to seventy-six in 1955, the UN membership had

▲ With United Nations secretary general Boutros Boutros-Ghali in his suite atop the UN building in New York (an association begun three decades earlier when lecturing together in France)

▲ *Conferencing with Senators Marcel Prud'homme, Pat Carney
and Emily McWhinney*

▲ *Fisheries consultations with UBC's Peter Pearse, minister of fisheries Fred Mifflin,
and former fisheries minister John Fraser*

▲ *Receiving the 1997 Aristotle Medal from Greek cabinet minister*
Filippos Petsalnikos on behalf of the government of Greece — with the citation:
"For his contribution to the progress of science, free thought and intellectual development
— values inextricably linked with Greek civilization throughout the years."

▲ *Addressing the crowd at the 1996 Vaisakhi parade in Vancouver's Punjabi market*

▲ *With Paul Martin and young Liberal supporters, 1999*

▲ *Remembrance Day service at UBC War Memorial, 1994*

▲ *Commission sur la langue française au Québec, (1968–1973): Nicolas Matesco-Matte, Madeleine Doyon-Ferland, Jean-Denis Gendron, Aimé Gagné, Edward McWhinney, Jean-Guy Lavigne (secretary).*

▲ BRAINS TRUST – Ontario premier John Robarts' advisory committee on Confederation, 1964–1971.
BACK ROW (L. TO R.): John Conway, George Gathercole, Bora Laskin, John Meisel, Ted McWhinney, Clifford Magone, T.H.B. Symons, Paul Fox, Roger Séquin. FRONT ROW (L. TO R.): Richard Dillon, Alexander Brady, J. Harvey Perry, H. Ian Macdonald (chair), Premier John Robarts, Eugene Forsey, W.R. Lederman, Donald Creighton, Rev. Lucien Matte.

▲ *Return courtesy call on the Prime Minister in his House of Commons office, 2001*

▲ *With Emily McWhinney*

already reached one hundred states by 1960, and was to mushroom further to 185 by the mid-1990s. New political alignments, logically linking the (in Cold War terms) non-aligned states outside the two blocks, Western and Soviet, emerged. From now on, and except perhaps within the Commonwealth, itself an organization of diminished political weight because of the proliferation of other competing power alignments, victories and breakthroughs in Canadian foreign policy would require hard work. Canada would be thrown back, more and more, on core associations to which it was historically tied, like the immediate postwar North Atlantic Treaty Organization (NATO) and the somewhat amorphous and open-ended "Western European and Others" (WEO) voting group operating within the UN general assembly. High posts within the UN secretariat and specialized agencies, and institutions such as the International Court of Justice, which had come to Canada almost as a matter of course in the late 1940s and 1950s, would now have to be lobbied for intensively. While support for the United Nations still would remain a cornerstone of Canadian foreign policy (and a principal talking point for Canadian political leaders), nevertheless with the retrenchment of opportunities for successful maneuvering, some of the earlier Canadian idealism may have been made to yield to conceptions of the national self-interest, narrowly construed.

One remembers Paul Martin, Sr., translated from the foreign ministry to the Senate after Trudeau's accession to office in 1968, as expressing his personal sadness as a lifetime student of the United Nations and the International Court of Justice, at the decision by then foreign minister Mitchell Sharp in 1970 to cut down on Canada's hitherto unqualified acceptance of the Court's jurisdiction in order to exclude any dispute covering Canada's new Arctic Waters Pollution Act. The justification advanced for this *volte-face* in traditional Canadian foreign policy was the suggested possibility, if Canada were to retain its original, unqualified acceptance of Court jurisdiction, that some other state might bring a successful action against Canada in the International Court! The substantive premise of the exclusion was, arguably from the viewpoint of existing international law and practice, at least questionable. It was a step backward. Joe Clark's short-lived Conservative government negated that particular negation in 1979 by quietly restoring Canada's original unqualified acceptance of the International Court's jurisdiction.

Under both the Mulroney and the Chrétien governments, the impact of the new continentalism opened up by Canada's adherence to the Canada-US bilateral free-trade agreement and to the Canada-USA-Mexico trilateral free-trade agreement has still to be fully comprehended and digested. A prime lesson from nineteenth- and twentieth-century European historical experience has been to validate Bismarck's thesis that customs unions and similar economic supranational affiliations are often but a step on the road to full political and constitutional-legal union. Given the speed with which the melding of Canadian financial and economic policies with US policies has proceeded and also the extent of the movement of trade and commerce across the common Canada-United States frontiers today, it is surprising how little attention has been given to the institutionalization of the new relations between the two countries.

Advanced institutional models might perhaps be suggested for some more substantial and more effective coordination or reconciliation of Canadian and US policies under the free-trade agreement and in the larger political domain that this trading partnership increasingly implies. One such example might be to create standing parliamentary delegations from the two countries, having official advisory or decisional competences, on the model of the Delegations from the Austrian and Hungarian parliaments, after the *Ausgleich* (union) of 1867, which essentially reconciled in constitutional-legal form two key nationalities within the Austro-Hungarian empire after generations of conflict. This solution has been a paradigm for comparative constitutional lawyers looking for institutional solutions for conflicts in plural-national societies.[82]

---

[82] It was briefly raised by Quebec jurist Jacques-Yvan Morin, in particular, in the early, heady days of Quebec's "quiet revolution" in the 1960s as a pos-

In terms of transnational association between sovereign states not yet ready or willing to go the "constitutional" route of the European Community (i.e., the states involved in the burgeoning continentalism in North America), it would appear as a positive idea for consideration. Another possibility would be to create a senior portfolio within cabinet for Canada-US relations, having priority over other ministries in terms of the regulation of bilateral Canada-US conflicts. In the special context of the post-September 2001 terrorist events, Chrétien moved part of the way to this in endowing his deputy prime minister, John Manley, with authority over transborder security issues, with the apparent power to coordinate and, if need be, to preempt action by other ministers.

This new continentalism does bring with it certain obligations of comity — of cooperation and mutual self-restraint in Canada-US relations. This implies settling differences by quiet diplomacy rather than rhetorical exchanges such as we have sometimes seen in recent years in the media and in public forums. These canons of comity may not always have been comprehended and acted upon by all the players. Sometimes, in Canada, we have seemed to act as if the golden era of Mike Pearson and Paul Martin, Sr., and of our erstwhile moral leadership role with third world and non-aligned countries was still with us, and available for invocation. With several multilateral treaty enterprises in which Canada has been engaged in recent years, and for the eventual completion and signature of which we were able to claim some special credit, some question of efficacy as law-in-action remained. One wonders whether, with a more consciously modest public role (and with more friendly persuasion in private with our key continental partner and also our most important European associates), we might have assured a more representative and more inclusive final treaty in terms of those states that were prepared, in the end, to sign on.

This question relates specifically to two recent multilateral

---

sible model for relations of the Quebec national assembly with legislatures in English-speaking Canada. However, the analogy was considered too remote for Canadian political facts at the time, and thus was dismissed.

treaties: the Rome statute on creation of an International Criminal Court, and the Land Mines treaty banning the use and also the manufacture and sale and export of these particularly cruel weapons of terror against civilian populations and military forces. Treated as "law-in-books" and for their moral and educational value, these treaties are admirable diplomatic efforts. But without all the principal political players likely to be involved in any concrete application of the treaties — the United States, Russia, China, France, Britain, all the permanent members of the security council — their operation as law-in-action would be severely diminished. Would relatively small concessions to the special sensitivities of our continental partner — perhaps as to the operational timing of certain clauses of the text, or allowing special exceptions where peace-enforcement action is taken under the prior, express legal authority of the UN security council or general assembly — have been a more helpful role for Canada in the diplomatic run-up to both treaties? The dilemma in choosing between an ideal text to which some states only, and not necessarily the key players, will agree to be bound, and a philosophically less coherent or satisfying document, which all players will accept, is real. In the examination of the oral testimony and evidence before the House of Commons committees charged with overseeing the two projects, the intermediate "third way" option was not raised by government or opposition party representatives, nor was it canvassed by the specialist witnesses brought in by the government in amplification or in support of its position.

A troubling question remains as to whether Canadian foreign policy and foreign policy makers in more recent years have not been infected with a gnawing form of anti-Americanism, as a sort of reverse reaction to the increasing absorption of Canadian industry and commerce into the larger decisions of the US private sector economy. Certainly, it was an ill-disguised secret that key Canadian officials, in the run-up to the 2000 presidential election in the United States, had expressed their preference for a win by the Democratic party candidate. This may explain some of President Bush's evident coolness toward Prime Minister Chrétien in the timing and place of the conventional public protocol gestures after the final outcome was decided.[83] One may wonder, again, how a Canadian ambassador to the United Nations (another career diplomat who normally would have known better) could excoriate the American president before the security council in New York on 11 July 2002 for failing to ratify the treaty on the International Criminal Court.[84] Canada was not, at the time, a member of the security council, and the language used should have been reserved for the foreign minister if the ambassador's words, in fact, reflected government policy. The minister, in that case, should make the statement himself and personally accept the political responsibility and any political fallout from it. The Athenian gadfly role, however, would seem better reserved for consciously and deliberately lesser state players, like Norway and Ireland, which, through a succession of very bright political leaders in recent years, have articulated successfully the more *avant-garde,* wave-of-the-future positions on the international rule of law.

Perhaps as a consequence of such evident coolness in Ottawa-Washington contacts, some of the breakthroughs in bilateral relations between the two countries have come, not through the formal diplomatic channels of communication between foreign ministry and state department, but in more informal arenas. The exchanges that take place in the Canada-US parliamentary friendship committee offer an example. There are also direct dealings between functionally based Canadian ministers and their US counterparts, or with US state governors or, in some cases, with the chairs of key US Senate or House committees. Such practice would correspond to the reality: the law-in-action of policy-making and its

---

[83] That is to say, the when and where of it, in terms of whether the Canadian PM would be the first foreign leader invited to meet the new president (as often had been the case in the past), and whether this meeting, whenever it did take place, would be at the White House or at his Texas residence (the apparent symbol of highest favour). Chrétien was to lose out on both counts.

[84] At the time, the US was in the company of China, India, Russia, Israel, and more than 100 other states that had not ratified this treaty.

effective location and distribution under the United States constitutional separation of powers. This is one of the arguments prompt-
ing the suggestion that Canada-US relations in future federal
governments be entrusted to a super-ministry, possibly under the
recently strengthened office of deputy prime minister. It would
have priority, where necessary, over other ministries. Finally, it
would be partly based in Washington, D.C., as well as in Ottawa.
The long, seemingly interminable delays in renegotiation of the
Pacific Salmon Treaty of 1985, which had bogged down in the foreign ministry's persistent emphasis on judicial settlement,[85] were
eventually effectively circumvented by direct initiatives from the
Canadian fisheries minister, David Anderson, with his US counterparts, and dealings, among others, with the key US Senators overseeing the president's files. It is a lesson in practical politics that
Canadian policy-makers of the 1950s and 1960s knew very well.
And it may have to be re-learnt if we are to make more substantial
progress on difficult files such as softwood lumber, where political
negotiating solutions, based on comity and reciprocity, offer prospects of quicker, more beneficial results than complex legal complaints and procedures and protracted litigation before the World
Trade Organization Tribunal and similar bodies.

At an even more practical, down-to-earth level (i.e., impacting
directly on the general public) the US administration's security
concerns in the aftermath of 11 September have had some immediate implications for Canada's continental role. The interests of
my constituents, for example, dictated that I give top priority to
promoting the free movement of goods, ideas and people across
the common frontier, and to removing unnecessary administrative
or security clogs.[86] In particular, when amendments to US immi-

---

[85] Anathema in US administration circles since Washington's withdrawal
from the compulsory jurisdiction of the World Court after its 1986 preliminary jurisdictional rulings against the US in *Nicaragua v. United States*.

[86] Vancouver Quadra is but an hour's drive by car from the US border, and
many of its residents travel frequently to and from the United States, as do
the representatives of Vancouver corporations and university faculty with
close trans-border commercial and other ties.

gration laws were introduced applying Draconian new controls that were clearly directed at US-Mexico border crossings, but which, of necessity under US constitutional law requirements, were formulated in general terms without geographical limits, I sought to make common cause with border-state US Senators and Congressmen in arguing for an administrative gloss on the new law that would allow for dispensation from the strict letter of the law at the Canada-US border. Suggestions of this nature, made without rhetorical flourishes, were fairly readily accepted and applied, quietly and without a public fanfare. Not to have done so would have been to have risked economic chaos on both sides of our common frontier.

After 11 September, there was a perception in Washington that some of the terrorist suspects had been able to enter the US from Canada because of lax security measures on the Canadian side, which included open-ended Canadian immigration laws, particularly those dealing with refugee claimants. Although any direct Canadian responsibility for these terrorist events was never established,[87] they brought into the open the case for a common North American security perimeter. This does not mean any necessary Canadian domestic application of US law or any uniformity between the two countries' laws, but would sensibly involve full coordination and cooperation in the administration and application of the two countries' laws. In the result, it does seem to have accelerated acceptance within the federal government of the need for a full-scale review of Canada's immigration laws, and to a correction, in particular, of gross abuses in refugee claim procedures and administration. Issues such as these have become part of the

---

[87] The example of terrorist Ahmed Ressam, who was convicted earlier in 2001 of plotting to bomb Los Angeles International Airport during millennium celebrations, lingered in the memories of United States officials, politicians, broadcasters and, no doubt, the public-at-large. Ressam, who had evaded deportation from Canada by exploiting all the loopholes in the Canadian refugee regulations before going underground, was caught attempting to smuggle explosives into the United States from British Columbia in December 1999.

mandate of the new minister in charge of security issues, Deputy Prime Minister John Manley. They would obviously become priority concerns of any future federal super-ministry on Canada-United States relations.

V

CROSSROADS

There are lessons from other countries that, in the last fifty years, have tried to change their constitutional systems in fundamental, far-reaching ways. Sometimes these exercises have been successful. More often they have ended in total failure. The lessons or "rules of prudence" for contemporary constitution-makers flow equally from both sets of experience. A first rule is that it is extremely difficult to secure substantial change in a country that is a genuinely viable concern, politically and economically. Political inanition reigns, however cumbersome and outmoded existing institutions and processes may be. The maxim, "if it isn't broken, don't try to fix it," is accepted as a warning to venturesome political leaders that they may act at their peril if they move at all. This is a principal lesson flowing from the successive failures in Canada of the Meech Lake and Charlottetown constitutional accords of the late

1980s and early 1990s. The political elite and its academic and information-media supporting cohorts may have been convinced of the need for change, but the general public was not. Overconfidence of the political elite led to failure to take on the job of educating the public on the need to make changes, before fundamental constitutional-governmental revision could sensibly be ventured upon.

A second rule is that it is normally only in times of public euphoria, following on some cataclysmic event — a successful political revolution, a great military victory (or even the mass emotion prompted by a national defeat) — that the necessary prior public consensus can be marshaled, and then maintained, to support a wholly new constitutional act or at least major alterations to an existing one. This has important implications as to the timing of any project of change. One must pluck the blossom of the day and act quickly, lest a fleeting public consensus dwindle away and be lost. General de Gaulle dallied a little too long after the liberation of France in 1944 in totally recasting the discredited Third Republic. This resulted in the weak compromises of the Fourth Republic in 1946. He made no similar mistake, however, with the constitution of the Fifth Republic, drafted and enacted in his own image in 1958, after the political collapse of the Fourth Republic. I always thought that Prime Minister Trudeau, following his brilliant pro-federalism victory in the 1980 sovereignty-association referendum campaign in Quebec, was too cautious in his attempt to fulfill his promise to remake the Canadian constitution. Indeed, his patriation project was neither comprehensive enough nor sufficiently exciting to capture and hold the initial public enthusiasm and support that in English-speaking Canada flowed from gratitude at Quebec voters' rejection of the sovereignty-association formula. There also is reason to believe that if Prime Minister Mulroney had acted quickly in following up the original Meech Lake Accord in 1987, instead of allowing the necessary constitutional-legal ratification by the provinces to drag on for three years, we might then have had a completed amendment of the constitution, rather than a constitutional near-miss. In each of these cases, the timing was right in the initial decision to launch constitutional change. It was in the follow-up, while that too fleeting initial consensus was still there, that the further lesson of moving quickly was lost.

Institutional Atrophy

The timing factor — the *When* — of constitutional change is linked to the further question of the justification for change — the *Why* — which must be brought out on a thoroughly empirical basis. The atrophy of key Westminster-style offices that were "received" with the original Constitution Act of 1867, is more and more visible, and it certainly has direct and continuing consequences for the effective functioning of the federal government and its main institutions. The "Passing of Parliament," already discussed, is a result of the sheer concentration of executive power today (itself a result of the unusual complexity of contemporary community decision-making) in its processes and also in the nature of the social and economic problems that have to be confronted and resolved. This has brought with it the massive delegation of authority from the executive to the bureaucracy, and the growth of an immense body of administrative law that seems incapable of adequate supervision and control by the ordinary courts. The European remedy of a special *droit administratif,* administered by a specialized judicial élite, the *Conseil d'Etat,* seems so far to have escaped us in Canada in spite of our dualist (French *droit civil* and English Common Law) legal inheritance.

The dilemma today is that, with the fairly continuous Canadian practice of electing majority governments, and with the House of Commons having no statutory fixed term independent from any executive power to cause a dissolution of Parliament, the House proceedings become totally dependent on the executive of the day. In fact, except for the daily question period, they take on the character of staged, ritualistic performances before an empty House. This is not a situation that encourages the best and the brightest younger talent to opt for a political career in preference to the temptations (and greater financial rewards) of business and commercial life.[88] The assorted constitutional correctives currently ventured by the think-tanks around Ottawa for breathing new life into the parliamentary system hardly seem anything more than the petit-point needlework of constitutional change. These recommendations include paying the chairs of the House's largely passive committees a modest additional annual stipend, or increasing still more the salaries and allowances of MPs or their already inflated parliamentary pensions. A special, extra-parliamentary task force composed of two very experienced and sensible ex-MPs from the Liberal and Conservative parties respectively, Ed Lumley and Jake Epp, suggested $9,480 per year as an extra bonus for standing committee or standing joint committee chairs. However, this bonus (which in 2002 amounted to $9,700) seems much too low when compared to that paid to "supporting players" like secretaries of state ($48,618 in 2002) to command any extra prestige.

The federal electoral system is anchored in single-member, geographically-based constituencies — the ultimate democratic principle. Unfortunately, this is tied to the first-past-the-post vote-counting rule, which may further discourage established professional talent from taking the plunge, politically, to run for election. This, of course, leaves out the pre-election hurdle of having to win a party nomination, which is difficult and expensive enough in itself.[89] The European *scrutin de liste* electoral system, under which all or at least some percentage of the members of the legislature are chosen according to preestablished lists of party candidates,

---

[88] Or the even greater contemporary challenge of moving permanently to the United States under the enormously facilitated rules and practices for such professional border-crossing that have grown up around the Canada-US Free Trade Agreement.

[89] It seems unacceptable in democratic terms to have the party leader bypass the party constitutional processes to appoint party candidates, as Prime Minister Chrétien has done frequently in Quebec and Ontario, and even, albeit on rarer occasions, in British Columbia and elsewhere.

with the resulting seats allocated on a proportional representation basis, does not appear to be acceptable in a Canadian political context. It leaves too much power to the party bureaucratic hierarchy in selecting candidates for the party list and establishing their ranking thereon. In practice, it is undemocratic. So is the expedient of recruiting "new blood" for the cabinet through appointment to the non-elected Senate. Cabinet ministers, by convention, are supposed to be answerable to the elected House of Commons on questions related to key government policy decisions, as is the prime minister. It is a tradition that is reinforced today by the perceived decline in the constitutional legitimacy of the Senate because of its appointed membership.

The best of the proposals for electoral reform, and least vulnerable to criticisms of constitutional illegitimacy, would be the Australian-style preferential voting system. In each single-member constituency, eligible voters rank (number) the candidate names on their ballots in order of preference (i.e., 1,2,3,4). When the votes are counted, candidates are progressively eliminated until one of them achieves an absolute majority. This is *so* obviously fair. Nevertheless, it is unlikely to be introduced in Britain and Canada, where governments have obtained, invariably, their parliamentary majorities on the first-past-the-post system with a simple plurality of votes cast.

The larger question still remains of whether the cabinet system, as such, is the best constitutional response to the needs of executive decision-making today. The qualities and the skills required to be a viable political candidate at the outset of the twenty-first century are intrinsically different from those of an executive. An intelligent, intellectually disciplined person, with proper application, may be able to acquire both sets of skills, but is it worth the effort? Is it worth the expenditure of extra time involved? As Jean Chrétien noted in his memoirs, *Straight from the Heart* (published while he was still in opposition in 1985), Mike Pearson, as prime minister, followed the classical British constitutional practice of trying, whenever possible, to have MPs serve an apprenticeship in junior governmental posts as parliamentary secretaries and the like, to test and develop their executive skills for potential later promotion to senior cabinet posts. Some, like the very able Donald Macdonald, had to put in their time in the trenches in this way.

Chrétien himself as prime minister, however, has hardly felt constrained by this practice. It has been one of the more obvious causes of sub-surface discontent within his caucus. Choosing those people one feels "comfortable" with by virtue of their demonstrated loyalty and capabilities in past leadership contests may be understandable enough for certain posts where the leader's full personal confidence is required, such as that of political minister for a particular region or province. But for the general range of executive appointments, the best and politically most acceptable criteria are provided by successful performance in prior posts in government or after having won one's spurs in business or professional life outside Parliament. The observable decline in the quality and range of experience of candidates for appointment to key executive posts in government is one of the more troubling political facts of life today. The St. Laurent, Diefenbaker, Pearson and Trudeau eras saw a rich range of executive talent in Parliament available for cabinet posts. The attractions outside Parliament only partly explain the gap in today's executive talent.

An obvious, macro-solution, which could only come as part of some future total revision of the constitution, would be to consider recognizing, as some other contemporary constitutional systems do, that executive power and legislative power are functionally distinct and require different skills, and that they would best be separated in the final constitutional-governmental system. We would be entering, then, upon a constitutional separation-of-powers, with an extended system of constitutional checks and balances between the coordinate institutions of government — executive, legislative and judicial. The United States constitution provides the best-known model, but there are others available that might just as well or better serve Canadian needs. The gap, in terms of relative prestige and power (to say nothing of status and financial emoluments) would also logically disappear between officeholders in the separate coordinate institutions. And why not, granted the equality of contribution of each institution in its own special constitutional sphere of operations? A United States Senator having the mandate of direct popular election, and particularly one who is also the chair of a key Senate committee, normally ranks in public standing and prestige, as well as in effective power, ahead of cabinet members (other perhaps than those in treasury, state and defence). The salary differential in the United States between Senators and cabinet ministers is insignificant, representing the constitutional-legal and also political realities that they bear equally (though functionally different and differentiated) the weight and responsibility of governance.

The atrophy of federal constitutional institutions and the withering away of the House of Commons in particular are not phenomena of recent origin, limited to or even created by the Chrétien government, but represent long-range changes in the roles and missions of Parliament and of the cabinet that were already in full evidence during the decade and a half of the Trudeau administration. In confirmation of this, I cite from my written conclusions given to the McGrath committee,[90] at its direct request, on 28 March 1985:

— the "presidentializing" of our system of government and its increasing approximation to various foreign models (US model, French model — Fifth Republic vintage) of strong executive government, separated from the legislature and legislative majorities, is continuing, and probably cannot usefully be reversed;

— our executive government no longer corresponds to the "classical" (nineteenth century) Westminster model of an English parliamentary executive. (For that matter, neither does Prime Minister Thatcher's government in Great Britain);

---

[90] A House of Commons committee on the "Reform of the House of Commons," created under the Mulroney government in 1985, and chaired by Conservative MP James McGrath.

— the loss by Parliament of "classical" Westminster-style functions and attributes has brought a certain dis-equilibrium in general constitutional forces, and brought a need for new essays in countervailing power (constitutional separation of powers).

My overall counsel to the McGrath committee then, as it would be today, was as follows:

the task of examining the desirable nature and character of Parliament today should be approached soberly, without too many inhibitions or preoccupations based on historical ideal-types or paradigms that have no foundation in contemporary practice.

While fundamental changes in the internal structure and institutional balance of the federal government are hardly likely to be on the operational agenda in the immediate future, there are other federal institutions from the nineteenth-century constitutional system that have been touched by the emergence of the new constitutional principle of legitimacy: that large discretionary decision-making powers in government should only be exercised by persons who have already been mandated by some form of public election process, direct or indirect. The Supreme Court of Canada, by events not of its own choosing and without being consulted, became effectively charged, in consequence of the enactment of the Constitution Act of 1982 and the Canadian Charter of Rights and Freedoms, with the overview and application and development of a vast new civil rights jurisprudence. For these unexpected changes, the past, rather narrowly defined jurisdiction of the Court (as well as the past professional training and experience of its individual judges) provided little in the way of practical lessons as to how best to handle cases with high political content, where judicial decisions inevitably would provoke political comment and criticism, and often strong community passions. The Supreme Court after 1982 was transformed in many respects into a *de facto* constitutional court, with obvious comparison to the role of the US Supreme Court since the time of the Judiciary Act reforms of 1925, and even more to the post-World War II European specialized tribunals.

The Court thus entered suddenly into the realm of judicial "leg-islation" before it had time to develop those canons of judicial self-restraint on "political questions." In the result, the Supreme Court of Canada has had to proceed by trial and error, with frequent difficulty in reaching surface consensus or in writing majority opinions that will provide at least a lowest-common-denominator of agreement in reasoned explanation and justification of the final ground of decision in a case. The sometimes colourful attacks on the Court and its judges within the House of Commons reflect resulting political tensions. In expert evidence to various parliamentary committees and royal commissions in the 1970s and the 1980s, I had suggested changes in the system of selection of the judges for the court, including the possibility of parliamentary participation in the executive selection process, or at least the holding of public hearings on candidates provisionally nominated by the executive. This could be done without the necessity of a parliamentary vote in ratification of any executive nomination to the Court. There is an emerging view that some such role might well be entrusted to a new, popularly elected Senate if such a constitutional reform were to be introduced. Without Senate reform, it would properly go to the House of Commons, where any such role, if it did not provide for ratification votes, would require neither constitutional amendment nor statutory change.

As for the Senate itself, it is at the core of much of the public discontent with the federal government (in addition to being at the forefront of public demands for fundamental change in federal institutions). One hears few good words about the Senate as it is presently constituted, and there is public anger at the perceived financial rewards for Senate members who are too easily lumped together and dismissed as political "patronage" appointments in these public criticisms. Yet the work of the Senate committees, particularly in the specialized areas of finance and banking, is of very high quality. The opportunity for extra leisure time for reflection, coming from never having to run for election or re-election and serving in a purely appointive post until an eventual compulsory retirement at seventy-five, undoubtedly helps. Inside the Canadian

Senate, a conscious application of a politic of self-restraint as to powers that, in terms of the Constitution Act as written, are coequal with those of the Lower House (with the exception of the intro- duction of money bills), has stemmed from a prudent recognition of the political limits of an unelected House. This conventional constitutional development reduces the risk of confrontation with the elected House of Commons.

With the British House of Lords, the Parliament Act of 1911, reinforced by the Parliament Act of 1949, has reduced, in positive law form, the once equal powers of the Lords with the Commons to a limited, suspensive veto only. This ensures, at worst, a delay of one year in any attempt by the Upper Chamber to frustrate the legislative will of a House of Commons majority. No such change in the positive law of the constitution has been made in Canada to reduce the Senate's legal competences. Contemporary practice, however, is clear. The Senate will act sensibly to allow further time for reflection and study in the case of any Commons bill that a Senate majority may feel is too hastily or sloppily drafted. But the Senate normally will not do much more than that. During my two terms in Parliament, the Senate several times intervened to ensure further time and opportunity for reflection on bills from the Com- mons — notably on the Newfoundland schools issue and on Aboriginal land treaties. There was some general feeling that the legislation in question benefited from further public hearings by the Senate and the incidental amendments that flowed from them. The Senate did not attempt to impose its will beyond that, and the bills, on return to the House of Commons, were duly enacted.

The affirmative case for the Senate — for an elected Senate — comes from recognition of a necessary regional/provincial bal- ance that a House selected on regional representational lines should have. Opposition, particularly in Western Canada, however, has focused on the completely outdated population lines on which the allocation of seats to the different regions within the Canadian federal system is made. Whatever the justification in the late nineteenth century, it is simply politically unacceptable today that, out of a total of one hundred and four seats in the Senate, Quebec and Ontario should each have twenty-four seats, and British Columbia only *six*. Nova Scotia and New Brunswick, with far less population than BC, each have ten seats. Tiny Prince Edward Island has four Senators. It is for this reason that many of those who argue for a reformed, elected Senate could not accept the federal opposition Reform party strategy of eventually reaching an elected Senate through direct election, as vacancies should arise in the future to the Senate, under the existing nineteenth-century regional-distribution formula. This would tend to legitimate a wholly illegitimate division of regional power within the Senate, and would amount to a constitutional negation of the principle of a representative institution.

There appears little chance of legally transforming the Senate unless we have a total constitutional revision in which a reformed and fairly elected Senate would be an integral part. Possibly we could persuade the Supreme Court of Canada to accept a challenge to the constitutionality of the Senate's basic composition. The constitutional amending machinery established under the Constitution Act of 1982 establishes too many and too complex legal barriers in the form of unanimity of the provinces, or at least special majorities of them, to believe that fundamental reform of the Senate can be accomplished by federal-provincial cooperative action under the constitutional amendment rubric. Governments at both levels, federal and provincial, however, are sensitive to the Senate's political vulnerability today, because of the undemocratic character of its composition and choice of members.

Prime Minister Mulroney, while ratification of the Meech Lake Accord was still open, acted in concert with Premier Bourassa to apply its formula to Senate appointments from Quebec. The Quebec government supplied the list of candidates from which the prime minister chose his appointees. It is generally agreed that the group of Quebec Senators so selected was the best qualified in a number of years. It included well-known constitutionalists Gérald

Beaudoin and Claire Kirkland-Casgrain. A number of prime ministers, including Brian Mulroney, have chosen their Senate appointees from persons who had already held elective federal offices in the House of Commons, and these appointments have been well received on the basis that those chosen had at least been through the electoral fires and proven themselves. Pat Carney and Gerry St. Germain, as Conservatives, and Ray Perrault and Len Marchand as Liberals — all from BC — come to mind. The most politically popular, at least most acceptable, category of Senate appointee, however, has turned out to be the senior citizens — a group Chrétien arrived at almost by chance during his first term by choosing several persons just short of their seventy-fifth birthday, the statutory retirement age of all appointees to the Senate. These senior citizens were informed, intelligent, articulate and well-spoken. The prime minister was delighted by the public's approval, and repeated the process. A number of very able seventy-three- and seventy-four-year-olds, who had never expected appointment and had certainly never asked for it, thus entered the Senate and were generally welcomed by their House of Commons colleagues. I am reminded, among others, of the Alberta educator Jean Forest.

In contrast, most public obloquy has been directed at those younger appointees to the Senate — people with many years to run on a relatively comfortable combination of salary and allowances (and as little work as they like) until they will reach the compulsory retirement age of seventy-five. Prime ministers add insult to injury in the public mind when they appoint men and women in their late thirties or early forties who have achieved very little in the way of proven public service or professional competence. A recent case that aroused great anger involved a Senator who spent his winters in residence at his luxurious Mexican villa, with only token visits to arctic Ottawa in between. Andrew Thompson had been a rather ineffectual Liberal leader of the opposition in the Ontario legislature while still in his thirties. He was forty-two when he was appointed to the Senate by Prime Minister Pearson (of all persons) in April 1967. Three decades later in March 1998, with a menace of expulsion from the Senate for reason of sustained absenteeism hanging over his head, he faxed in his resignation, and conserved his Senate retirement privileges.[91]

Decline in Public Respect

The "respect" factor is easy enough to identify in its negative consequences and in the contributing causes, multiple as these are now. It is much harder to offer correctives that are meaningful and also politically realizable. As earlier noted, there is an observable decline in the quality and the range of expertise of persons prepared to offer themselves as party candidates, and a resulting even more marked decline in the pool of talent available within the House of Commons for cabinet building. The prospects are simply too chancy in Canada under the Westminster-style parliamentary executive to attract or retain people in middle age and at the height of their professional careers. This is in contrast to the situation in the United States, where high-powered executives are clearly moved to take leave to go to Washington to serve for the usual two- or four-year stints in the cabinet or similar high executive post before returning to their former private lives.

One remembers the case of Art Phillips, the first of that bright, attractive and articulate class of young mayors, who were elected in the great cities of Canada in the 1970s on a platform of large scale reform and modernization, and who were consciously and completely free of the taints of patronage and influence-peddling associated with big city politics in earlier times. Phillips was persuaded by the Trudeau recruitment scouts to accept the Liberal party nomination in Vancouver Centre in 1979, at a time when the

---

[91] Just before the end of my first term as an MP, Peter Bosa, a respected Ontario Senator, asked me if I would allow him to propose my name to the prime minister to replace Len Marchand, who was known to want to retire. He said the government had been in need of a constitutionalist since Eugene Forsey's retirement some years earlier. I respectfully declined: having just been elected, I could not now accept a non-elected parliamentary post.

Liberals were short of representation and new talent in the West. Of course Phillips won his seat, but the Liberals lost the election nationally that May, and had to give way to Joe Clark's minority Conservative government. Recruited as new front-bench executive talent for a government in office that was assumed to be about to be reelected, Phillips found himself with little or nothing to do of practical importance, as an ordinary MP in opposition. He consented to run for re-election after the Clark government fell in December, but his heart was obviously not in it and he lost. He never went back. A different constitutional system, with the executive divorced from the legislature, would be an obvious corrective.

Partial remedies have been tried by various incumbent governments to strengthen the executive talent so obviously lacking in cabinet. I've mentioned the method by which party hopefuls are directly appointed to a nomination in a safe seat without their having to run the gauntlet of contesting and winning their constituency's endorsement. On other occasions, a sitting MP is induced to vacate his or her seat with the offer of reward in some diplomatic, judicial or other public posting. But these devices raise too many objections, legal and other, in terms of democratic constitutionalism to be persisted in much longer. Again, an election law-based option borrowed from the European practice of reserving a percentage (perhaps half) of the seats in elections for the Lower House for candidates supplied on lists by the competing parties would certainly facilitate entry of able (but presumably not easily electable) executives from private life. But, as I've already observed, it would, at the same time, immensely increase the power of the nonelected party bureaucracies, and seems contrary to Canadian community expectations as to the democratic basis of parliamentary representation.

The alternative challenges, outside political life, for intellectually creative and energetic young people who have graduated from colleges and professional schools and have passed their first ten or fifteen years of professional apprenticeship, seem much greater today and also more attractive in terms of power (i.e., participation in the key decisions affecting society). The end of the Cold War has meant the increasing replacement of the erstwhile political-military premise of world order by an economic one, in which the main arenas become financial, and the main instruments and institutions are transnational or multinational corporations and trade and industry associations. The movement to abolition of frontiers and to free movement of goods and services within ever larger and more inclusive regional economic blocs in Europe and the Americas has strengthened and encouraged this perceptible shift in career orientation and goals from political to economic ones. Service in national public life doesn't have the same allure it once had. The negative images of actual behaviour in national political institutions, diffused over the national and international communication networks, have contributed to this turning away from national political outlets.

Some of the recent events in our own Parliament, in the manner of their execution much more perhaps than in their substance, appear in retrospect as self-inflicted wounds. I thought the controversy over augmenting the pensions of MPs and Senators during the first Chrétien mandate was not well handled, although the fault would appear to have been with the party whips and House leaders on both the government and opposition sides of the House, and not with the government and opposition leaders themselves. The parliamentary pensions scheme as it then existed, with the Canadian taxpayer contributing almost eight dollars for each single dollar contributed by individual MPs or Senators, was hard to defend. We all had a flood of angry letters from constituents about this, and harsh editorial comment from media around the country. A perfectly sensible suggestion from Reform MP Jim Silye, a young self-made millionaire and ex-Calgary football star, for getting Parliament out of the pension scheme altogether or at least reducing the pension plan to ordinary business, contributory principles,[92] and balancing this change by a substantial parliamen-

---

[92] One-on-one, in terms of government and MP/Senator contributions.

tary salary increase (with elimination of all hidden benefits), was laughed out of existence. When asked for a figure for his clean, no-hidden-benefits salary, Silye suggested $130,000. The figure was, in simple public relations terms in a time of extreme budget austerity, much too high, and yet it is not too far from the salary figure adopted by Parliament in 2001 at the beginning of Chrétien's third term. These latest changes, however, also retain various hidden benefits as to housing and the like from the earlier system which used to be justified, when they were inserted in the plan, as necessary because the public would not like direct salary increases.

The objections to the changes made in 2001 go also to the manner of their adoption. They were introduced within a few short months of the preceding general elections, but were never mentioned in the election campaign. And they were adopted after the elections, with extreme haste, in the final week of the parliamentary session before both Houses went off for the long summer break. There were several scant days only between first introduction of the bill in the Commons and its passage, and thus, no doubt designedly, there was no opportunity for public reaction. The contrast for the general public between the MPs and Senators rushing through, with virtually no debate or criticism, a measure concerning their personal financial well-being and welfare, and the sustained non-action by Parliament on several major bills before the House for some months, which were not adopted before the recess, was simply too stark. These new parliamentary salary increases were also made retroactive to the beginning of the year. The emerging consensus is that any further increases in parliamentary salaries and pensions should only be enacted with a provision that they not take effect until after the next general election so that the electors will have opportunity to vote their pleasure or displeasure.

One of the more positive steps taken by the Chrétien government following the 1993 election was to attempt to prevent, in advance, public scandals — in particular the allegations of conflict-of-interest and influence-peddling that had rocked earlier administrations and brought about the resignations, under fire, of cabinet ministers facing such charges. The government introduced special conflict-of-interest control legislation, creating the office of federal ethics commissioner, reporting directly to the prime minister. Each appointee to government office — minister, secretary of state, parliamentary secretary — now would be required to make full disclosure in writing to the ethics commissioner as to personal financial holdings and those of any spouse and immediate family. Somewhat more vaguely, each appointee had to provide full disclosure as to personal affiliations with non-governmental organizations, public interest associations, special interest groups and other private organizations. The first ethics commissioner was a semi-retired federal civil servant; his staff was small (so far as one could gather, only one other full-time professional officer); and the time-window for fulfilling the public disclosure obligation was minuscule, for in theory disclosure would have to coincide with the acceptance of the appointment, normally effective from the day of its public announcement.

As a parliamentary secretary, first in Fisheries and then in Foreign Affairs, I had myself to comply with the new law.[93] On the financial disclosure obligations, there were two options: first, to publish immediately, and to keep updated thereafter, a full list of all assets and holdings, of oneself and one's family: house, furniture, automobile, and all the personal property (stocks and shares, bonds, annuities, trust holdings, every form of financial benefit). The alternative disclosure option was to choose to go into a blind trust, under which one's own and one's family's total portfolio would be delivered to a trust company for its sole legal management and control. In this option, there was to be absolutely no communication between the trustee and oneself or one's family other than a bald statement, every three months, of the total value of the portfolio at that particular time. There would be no disclosure of the number or value of individual buying-and-selling transactions within the portfolio, or advice of the investment policies

---

[93] When I met with the new ethics commissioner, the time frame for compliance became effectively even more diminished by the fact that he was about to leave for a conference of ethics commissioners in Australia and that my disclosure would all have to be completed before he left.

behind such transactions until the blind trust should finally be terminated at the conclusion of one's government appointment.[94]

On what might be called, loosely, the public and special interest affiliation disclosure obligation, there was a lengthy (several hours) meeting between the ethics commissioner and myself, during which it became clear that, lacking any clear criteria in the federal law to guide the operation, one should disclose everything. This meant, in my own case, with professional and scientific ties going back to my student days in a number of different countries, a rather elaborate memory recall of committees, clubs, institutes and professional groups that I had once been invited to join and had never (through politeness or simple neglect) dropped. The search, apparently, was designed to identify extra-parliamentary social, religious, cultural and other ties that conceivably might influence one's attitude to future legislation. There were two specialist Canadian organizations in one of my fields of expertise — international law — to which I still belonged. One was the International Law Association (Canadian Branch), which had been at the leading edge of policy discussion and debate in such various fields as détente, nuclear disarmament, international terrorism, and international monetary and banking law. The second was the more recently formed Canadian Council on International Law, an association mainly of federal civil servants, Canadian military, and those Canadian academics and others working closely with the government on legal research contracts and the like. Since the obligation of disclosure had, as correlative requirement, one's resignation from organizations deemed in a political "conflict" situation with government policy-making, I agreed, under advice, not to leave the International Law Association but to resign from the (in my view politically much blander and uncontroversial and normally sympathetic to government policies) Canadian Council on

---

[94] It would appear from recent press reports and opposition party charges that there were somewhat more flexible arrangements for cabinet ministers such as the foreign affairs minister, William Graham, and former finance minister Paul Martin.

International Law. I also resigned from the World Federalists of Canada and the United Nations Association. Since leaving the government, I have rejoined a couple of these organizations. I have wondered if this exercise was really necessary in the public interest, or whether the system did not merely create the public illusion of removing potential conflicts-of-interest at the expense of substance. The alternative of introducing sharper, more precise sanctions under the Canadian criminal code with the intention of enforcing them in appropriate cases, as in the US and other countries, needs to be considered.

On the financial disclosure front, I opted, after full discussion with my wife (a professional economist and former financial consultant), to follow the blind trust course. We did this because of our experience in administering our own small personal investment portfolios and also a nonprofit, charitable education trust foundation that I had established and directed on a non-salaried basis in recent years. The weight of such administration was considerable, involving as it did almost daily communication with brokerage firms and financial houses and the very frequent trading of stocks and shares. The systematic reporting of every fresh financial transaction, as it might occur, to the ethics commissioner's office would add a still further burden, in time and stress, that could not easily be combined with the obligations of a government post superimposed on existing responsibilities as an MP. In opting for the blind trust, we did not receive any concrete advice or guidance from the ethics commissioner as to how to proceed. Indeed, his expertise seemingly lay elsewhere than in the financial part of his mandate. His office had no written guidelines; no model contracts; no short list of recommended and previously screened trustees; no system for monitoring the performance of the blind trust; and no remedies or remedies process. One was left on one's own.

I had been a shareholder, albeit a modest shareholder, in one of Canada's major chartered banks, and we chose one of the spinoffs from that firm's entry into the financial investment industry as our blind trustee. We were not happy with their concrete record of performance and administration when we were finally able, after I left the government, to gain access to the detailed record of sales and purchases and trading generally exercised by them in their capacity of blind trustees. A major national tax accounting firm confirmed our conclusions and reservations. I did not think that exposure to personal financial hazards should be a condition or consequence of holding a government post and, after finding other MPs had experienced similar difficulties, I raised the general principle with the prime minister. He, in turn, referred me to his deputy PM, Herb Gray. Gray suggested that, as a preliminary, I should invoke the bank's own well-advertised internal review system, which it describes as a bank ombudsman process, and which is itself subject to another internal banking review process, the Canadian bank ombudsman. Two years were spent in this process without any result. I had no doubt of the personal integrity and general good faith of the banks and banking officials involved. My impression that they may have moved too quickly, and without thinking through the need for adequate administrative-legal controls when venturing into the investment services industry, seemed confirmed in conversations with their chief executives in June 1998 on the larger issue of the then proposed bank mergers.[95]

Needless to say, I was not too satisfied as to the functioning of the federal ethics commissioner in the area of oversight and monitoring of my private financial activities. That said, a principal responsibility must remain with the government for its failure to define more fully the ethics commissioner's mandate, or to provide his office with the technical staff adequate — in numbers, range and depth of professional qualifications — to fulfill this review function. As it now stands, it remains an office without teeth,

---

[95] The proposed bank mergers were clearly headed for political failure at that moment, although their macro-policy objectives were clear enough and could be defended positively enough on a basis of the need of the Canadian banks to compete in a continental North American context with their US counterparts, which operated with no such legal restrictions as to merger under US law. The Canadian banks lost, then, because of their failure to consult enough at the political grassroots level and to enlist support from MPs who were being bombarded with complaints from local communities

since it has no real enforcement remedies. Perhaps, again, the simplest and most direct solution would be to approach its general mandate in the context of substantially revised and strengthened amendments of the Canadian criminal code imposing direct liability on government members for conflict-of-interest delinquencies.

The office of the ethics commissioner came under public and parliamentary attack on other grounds in the early part of Chrétien's third term as PM. In particular, it was contended that because the ethics commissioner reported directly to the prime minister and not to Parliament, he was not really independent. The current changes proposed for improving the office in response to this criticism seem but modest and incremental.

Escaping the Constitutional Straitjacket

Should there ever be agreement on the need for constitutional-governmental change, as such, and if the crucial timing factor also should be resolved, the question remains of how it can be done. The necessary legal starting point for all this is Part V, "Procedure for Amending Constitution of Canada," sections 38–49, in the Constitution Act of 1982. Adoption of an autonomous, all-Canadian, constitutional amending machinery had been one of the three elements of Trudeau's constitutional project. The enactment of the Constitution Act of 1982 achieved the objective of replacing the old imperial British route for amending the Canadian constitution by way of special legislation of the Parliament at Westminster, enacted at the request of the Canadian government. In

---

that feared the closing-down of banking facilities in their constituencies. Whatever the personal views, at the time, of the prime minister and the federal finance minister, the banks' merger proposals failed because of the resistance of rank-and-file MPs in caucus. The banks had signally failed to lobby and educate individual MPs as to the merits of their cause, and had over-estimated the will of government ministers to deliver on a potentially unpopular cause. In October 2002, Prime Minister Chrétien vetoed similar bank merger proposals, after his new finance minister, John Manley, had seemed to favour reopening the files.

symbolic terms, Canadian sovereignty was vindicated. But the price paid has been replacement of a highly flexible amending system that operated easily and quickly in modern times at the simple request of the federal government, with an extremely complicated and, in the end, almost totally rigid constitutional system.[96]

In comparative constitutional-legal science, one of the most popular ways of breaking out of constitutional straightjackets such as this is by resorting to the ultimate source of power — constituent power — usually involving recourse to the people, at some stage, for direct popular ratification or endorsement. The classic examples are to be found in the constitution-making of the French revolutionary and Napoleonic eras. Constitutional charters that then affirmed, in their own texts, that they were legally immutable and incapable of change; or less than that, that they were legally capable of change only after a certain, prescribed number of years, were replaced easily and quickly enough, when a felt necessity to do so had emerged, by a fresh act of constituent power. This was usually followed immediately by direct popular approval in a referendum held on the new charter. Plebiscitarian democracy requires, to be accepted as effective as law-in-action, a sufficiency of popular acceptance.

One might follow the lead of the politically cautious approach of the Supreme Court of Canada in its 1998 advisory opinion on the secession of Quebec, and decline to specify just what sort of numerical majority should be constitutionally sufficient. Obviously, it would have to be more than fifty percent, and would also have to have a certain regionally based character. One does not foresee

---

[96] In default of any easy amending machinery, even where there may be strong evidence of a large and broad national support for specific change or changes, Canadian political leaders have had to turn to tactical campaigns, or rely on tolerated practice, or glosses on the original Constitution Act of 1982 as written, under the name of customs or conventions of the constitution. The latter are most effective in the sphere of federalism and inter-governmental relations, assuming the support of the governments affected is there. They are less effective in other domains, however, unless they are, by nature, of little practical significance or importance and therefore not likely to be politically contested.

such a situation existing at the present time, or in the immediately foreseeable future. But resort to ultimate, constituent power must remain as an option, if the strains of adjusting antique federal constitutional machinery and processes inherited from 1867 (as well as the prior high political compromises from which they flowed) to the social and economic realities of contemporary Canada should become pathological and politically nontolerable on that account. The starting point of any constitutional system, in classical legal theory, is always a prior, meta-legal political fact, from which the legal rules and the public order system are subsequently derived. At some later stage, a new and more confident, pluralist Canadian society may want to detach itself from the Westminster-style model and start afresh, as many other mature industrial societies were able and willing to do in the reaction against the deemed failures of their own pre-World War II constitutional-governmental systems. It will be much harder to do it in Canada, but the option must surely exist. It would have to come from some sort of directly elected, national constituent assembly, with a very short time limit — one or two months — for reporting, and then followed by approval in a national referendum. The skills of political compromise in building the necessary plural regional consensus in support of any fundamental new steps in the constitution would be at a premium.

Politic of Little Steps

The obvious way — the logical way — to proceed to constitutional change today in the absence of any popular national consensus in support of total revision of the constitution is to concentrate on specific change in response to specific problems.[97] This was clearly Prime Minister Chrétien's preferred approach. Not seeing either a popular consensus in support of fundamental change or any need

---

[97] On a necessarily piecemeal basis under the complex and detailed formulae for constitutional amendment set out in Part V, sections 38–49, of the Constitution Act of 1982.

for specific changes, he applied a politic of *attente* and of resting with the status quo. Even with Quebec and the French fact in Canadian federalism — the preemptive constitutional concern, to the exclusion of all others, of all Canadian federal governments since the early 1960s — the federal politic has remained reactive since the spectacular failures of Meech Lake and Charlottetown. Federal responses have been essentially tactical political ones, without any new concrete proposals. The fact remains that many of the current proposals for change could, from the purely techni-cal-legal, constitutional viewpoint, still be accommodated or achieved within the difficult new constitutional amendment for-mulae established under the Constitution Act of 1982.

As to the possibility of venturing on a constitutional separation-of-powers (i.e., separating the federal executive or cabinet from the federal Parliament), the office of prime minister and the insti-tution of the cabinet are, of course, wholly customary; that is, they are conventional constitutional institutions, not part of the 1982 Constitution Act. Since this concerns only the executive govern-ment and the Parliament of Canada, there appears to be nothing to impede Parliament acting alone to deal with the issue, in accor-dance with Section 44 of the Constitution Act. The late Senator Eugene Forsey, our eminent constitutional scholar, once reminded me that until 1931 (under what was probably a mistaken interpre-tation of the constitutional law of the day) federal MPs had to resign their seats upon appointment to the cabinet.[98] Any step, by federal legislation, toward a full separation-of-powers, that involved liberating ministers from the necessity of obtaining election to Parliament, would amount to a constitutional revolution in its own right, with far-reaching implications for many other parts of the constitution. Examining it now as a hypothetical choice may help open the way to other approaches to modernization of the execu-

---

[98] The rule that no person could hold an office of emolument under the crown and remain a member of the House of Commons came into being in sixteenth-century England to guard against MPs being brought under the executive control of nefarious monarchs.

tive decision-making arm of government, and of the modes of recruitment of executive members — perhaps through changes in the electoral system. An interesting beginning, in recognition of the sharply augmented continentalization of post-NAFTA, post-September 11 federal decision-making, might be to station an important Canadian cabinet minister in Washington, D.C., independent of conventional foreign ministry processes and reporting directly to the prime minister at all times.

The Liberal premier of British Columbia, Gordon Campbell, elected in May 2001, opened up potential new dimensions for executive-legislative relations within the provincial government by promptly moving to implement an election promise to introduce a fixed, four-year term for the legislature, and a fixed quadrennial election date (mid-May in the fourth year of any mandate). This will certainly give more security to individual elected members of the provincial legislature *vis-à-vis* the provincial cabinet, and establish a certain independence from arbitrary or capricious use of the constitutional right of a premier to ask for (and in modern times to compel) an earlier dissolution of the legislature by the lieutenant governor. I am not sure if all of the constitutional implications of this provincial innovation have been fully considered, but some of the remaining issues — what happens, for example, if in midterm a government is defeated on a confidence issue because of internal party revolt — have proved easy to handle in cognate constitutional systems, and could be dealt with now, in advance, by legislation wholly within the constitutional competence of the province. The four-year constitutional limit, once announced, seemed to be welcomed generally. It is unlikely that any future provincial government would dare attempt to retreat from it. There is no doubt, however, of the constitutional competence of the province to enact a quadrennial legislature act, under section 45 of the Constitution Act of 1982.

Another important area had been touched on by the new BC premier in his 2001 election campaign, and thoroughly discussed in various expert commission reports (including the several reports of the FCM[99] task force on the constitution published during the constitutional round of the early 1980s). The province, acting alone under section 45 of the Constitution Act of 1982, would appear to have full capacity to endow municipalities with a special constitutional status in their own right, as recommended in the FCM reports. Such status could include, among its attributes, the power to amend their municipal charters; power to make rules, having the force of provincial law, within provincial lawmaking powers under the Canadian Constitution Act; and most importantly in a political sense, power to levy new forms of taxation, again within provincial powers under the Constitution. This would not, of course, be a substitute for some much more far-reaching constitutional revision, necessarily involving the federal government, and establishing some form of tri-level, federal system (federal-provincial-municipal), with direct participation of the municipal governments in existing federal-provincial tax-sharing and revenue agreements. The great metropolitan concentrations of population and resources are the location of most of the key social problems in Canada, and they have also been the main receiving centres for the new immigrant communities that are transforming the cultural, and also ultimately the political life of Canada today. Provincial action within provincial powers under the constitution might accelerate complementary federal action.

As previously observed, the most frequent publicly demanded area for constitutional change in Canada concerns the Senate. Unfortunately, one does not see any immediate prospects of fundamental change here. Incremental change proposals might include having individual provinces move to "elect" their own Senate candidates in the hope of persuading the federal prime minister to appoint any persons so endorsed by provincial electors, as Mulroney did in 1990 with Reform party candidate, General Stanley Waters from Alberta. And we have noted Mulroney's somewhat similar, once-in-a-lifetime gesture to Quebec in appointing Sen-

---

[99] Federation of Canadian Municipalities. See p. 31.

ators only from a list presented to him by the provincial premier. Measures such as these nevertheless may prove to be constitutional steps *backward,* so far as they serve to legitimate this institution's numerical status quo. It would seem better to wait on some more far-reaching reform. Under sections 42(1) and 38(1) of the Constitution Act of 1982, this would require the endorsement of at least seven out of the ten provinces, including in this number either Quebec or Ontario, in addition to federal parliamentary approval. Conceivably, correction of this glaring gap in the constitution could come only as part of a total constitutional revision, for which Quebec support might be sought in return for concessions that included (in the spirit of Pepin-Robarts) a requirement, in any Senate vote touching on the status of the French language and culture in Quebec, a concurrent (or double) majority — a majority of the Senate as a whole as well as a majority of the Quebec Senators. This, however, would be difficult to sell to the rest of Canada.

It is often forgotten that the emerging public consensus on constitutional change in the 1970s was broad enough to include the possibility of abolishing the Senate altogether. Indeed, this option was part of Trudeau's Constitutional Amendment bill in 1978, which lapsed with the dissolution of Parliament in the spring of 1979. The matter, however, in the meantime had been referred to the Supreme Court of Canada for an advisory opinion on its constitutionality — something the Court proceeded to render in December 1979, notwithstanding that it had become academic with the electoral defeat of the Trudeau government the previous May. In strict legal terms, the case might properly have been dismissed as "moot." At that stage, the Supreme Court had not yet been converted into the *de facto* special constitutional court that it was to become by virtue of the Constitution Act of 1982. It was manifestly inexperienced in handling high "political questions," but still it moved where Angels and constitutionalists might prudently have hesitated to tread, and rendered judgment.

It cited the role of the Senate in the "preservation of the rights of minorities," a Court observation that suggests the judges did not see fit to distinguish between the law-in-books of 1867 and the rather more contemporary, supervening law-in-action. The Court concluded that the constitution must "contemplate the continued existence of both the Senate and the House of Commons" and that it was beyond the competence of the Parliament of Canada to abolish the Senate; or to change its name; or to change the proportions of representation of the different provinces so as to correspond to changes in the population distribution; or to provide for the direct election of all or part of the Senate (as the Court said: "a radical change in the nature of one of the component parts of Parliament"). The Court further rejected, "with repugnance," any proposal to reduce the Senate's powers of veto over bills passed by the House of Commons and to confine it, instead, to a limited "suspensive veto" only, on the pattern of the dramatic curtailment of the hereditary British House of Lords veto power over the House of Commons that had been successfully enacted by the British Parliament sixty-eight years earlier in the Parliament Act of 1911.

The question referred to the Supreme Court had been formulated by Prime Minister Trudeau's erudite justice minister of the day, Otto Lang, who had also sponsored the Constitutional Amendment bill in the House. It was a brave attempt by the Trudeau government to effect a meaningful and timely constitutional reform. The ruling by the Supreme Court of Canada in *Reference re Legislative Authority of Parliament to Alter or Replace the Senate* stands perhaps more as a commentary on the limits of the constitutional thinking of the Supreme Court bench of the day, whose *per curiam*[100] opinion was developed and written during the prolonged absence, because of serious illness, of Chief Justice Bora Laskin, who did not return until the eve of the announcement of the decision. This ruling should not, I think, be regarded as a definitive disposition of the issues raised. One might hope for a federal justice minister, with the intellect, wit and imagination displayed in vain by Otto

---

[100] Unsigned opinion rendered by the whole court.

Lang two decades ago, to challenge the Court to try anew for a ruling more in line with contemporary political and constitutional reality.

Continental European jurisprudence in the immediate post-War years was intellectually stirred in reaction to the excesses of the erstwhile totalitarian regimes by notions of "unconstitutional constitutional norms." This meant that legal provisions, even in the constitutional charter itself, that run counter to the elemental principles of justice as viewed by contemporary society may become unconstitutional by that very fact. It is a constitutional negation to have a legislative chamber that is not mandated and legitimated by popular election. At some stage, it might be worth making a new approach to the Supreme Court for such a ruling, with the further suggestion that the Court might then be invited, following the pattern of rulings made by constitutional tribunals elsewhere, to announce its ruling, but to indicate at the same time that the Court would postpone its coming into effect for a certain definite period, say one or two years to allow all parties to come up with some new Upper House structure and form rather more compatible with the constitutional principles of a representative, free democratic society. (There would be nothing, of course, to prevent members of the present, purely appointive Senate becoming candidates for election to a new and restructured body. On their records, many would warrant party designation, and those with prior experience as MPs could probably be elected.)

VI

〜〜〜

LEADERSHIP
PERSONALITY VARIABLES

Chrétien Views his Office

Clues as to Chrétien's personal conception of his role in the federal constitutional system, and particularly in the largely unwritten, customary or conventional part not to be found in the Constitution Act of 1867, are contained in his memoir, *Straight from the Heart*. First published in 1985, it was written a few months after the Liberal government's defeat in the general elections of 1984 (which had followed on the heels of Chrétien's own loss to John Turner in the Liberal party leadership convention). First and most obvious is that Chrétien's prime interest and concern in politics is the interaction and competition of personalities, and not of policies or philosophical ideas. This conforms to the general public impression of him and his political style. It is clear that Chrétien derives a genuine joy from direct personal combat, whether on the electoral hustings or in Parliament itself. Others like Mike Pearson visibly shrank from person-to-person confrontations, and this was particularly observable in his direct clashes with John Diefenbaker in the House. Pierre Trudeau would become frustrated and irritated with personal exchanges, and he showed this readily enough in his responses inside the House and outside.

There is, however, another interesting element in Chrétien's character, and that is the absence of lasting personal political animosity after, though only after, a battle has been fought and won. This was in full evidence in the considerate and graceful way Chrétien treated Lucien Bouchard in the House, after Bouchard's sudden, near-fatal illness, and also after Bouchard announced his decision to quit federal politics to go back to Quebec as premier. A similar personal generosity and magnanimity, transcending conventional party lines or past political conflict, may be seen in his non-publicized personal telephone call to BC ex-premier Glen Clark after his complete acquittal on conflict-of-interest charges related to his term of office. He also called BC Premier Gordon Campbell during the media uproar resulting from the premier's drunk driving charge in Hawaii. The several public occasions outside Parliament of anger on Chrétien's part — when he turned upon civilian protesters and others — seemed out of character. I think they were attributable more to jet lag and travel fatigue resulting from an overly zealous personal staff's insistence on returning him immediately to his regular daily schedule without any break, after one or more weeks of exhausting international travel through a number of different time zones.

Chrétien's approach to internal politics of the federal Liberal caucus reflected his emphasis on personal ties, rather than any deep philosophical commitment to one camp or another in the very rare internal debates in caucus on policy issues, both large and small. His first real government post had been parliamentary secretary to Mitchell Sharp in 1966–1967, when Sharp was finance minister in the Pearson government.[101] Sharp, as Chrétien has noted, was clearly of the sober right-wing of the party on fiscal and financial issues, in marked contrast to the intellectually more innovative and politically more progressive Walter Gordon. Chrétien's personal ties to Mitchell Sharp remained long, long after Sharp's retirement from politics. Sharp was consulted on the formation of the Liberal cabinet in 1993, as well as on policy priorities, fiscal and other, for the new government. He was no doubt an important contributing factor in the essentially cautious, non-innovatory approach that, from the beginning, characterized the first Chrétien ministry.

The first Chrétien cabinet was to include Ron Irwin and David Dingwall, both former parliamentary secretaries to Chrétien, who (not surprisingly, for this was the key to some otherwise odd cabinet choices) had been very active in Chrétien's party leadership campaigns in 1984 and 1989. David Dingwall was very able. Apart from Paul Martin and John Manley, Dingwall and Doug Young were perhaps the best prepared, among ministers charged with the larger, functionally based departments, in digesting and analyzing the files and reaching a technically based decision which they could carry with confidence through cabinet committees and ultimately to the first minister. But their prior personal bond to the party chief and prime minister was clearly decisive in their making what Chrétien called his Team A, rather than his Team B.

Chrétien is patently uncomfortable in operating in the world of abstract ideas. He may have experienced difficulties in adjusting to the rarified intellectual atmosphere of the federal Liberal caucus of the Trudeau era, where the Quebec regional caucus of which he was, of course, a member, was stocked with fluently bilingual people with advanced graduate and professional degrees from the best schools in Europe or the United States, in addition to their Canadian qualifications. It was sometimes observed that these

---

[101] His earlier, short stint as Pearson's parliamentary secretary, beginning in the summer of 1965, was largely honorific (as this position invariably is), and no doubt doubly so because of the advent of the general election that fall.

"patrician" Quebecers not merely spoke Parisian French, but that they often spoke the "Queen's English" better than anglophone MPs in the Commons. Chrétien manifestly did not have the support of the Quebec "patrician" group during the 1984 leadership race. Their support went to other candidates — principally to John Turner, even if not necessarily with any positive enthusiasm on their part for Turner himself. They were simply against Chrétien. Chrétien indicates some sadness at this, particularly about Marc Lalonde, whose support he considered pivotal in rallying Quebec caucus support for himself in the Trudeau succession struggle. Chrétien nevertheless experimented with several of his own directly appointed Quebec "patrician" MPs for his cabinet during his first term (1993–1997). However, by the end of the 1990s, he was opting for more down-to-earth and younger Quebecers in Martin Cauchon and Denis Coderre, whom he personally selected and parachuted into very safe Liberal seats in metropolitan Montreal. They, of course, as young Liberals had worked in his party leadership campaigns.

Chrétien came from a large family whose parents had made the sacrifices necessary to carry their children on to higher education, and he has been rightly proud of his older brother, Maurice, and his younger brother, Michel, who went on to become medical practitioners and scientific researchers of recognized merit. In his private conversations, he would often refer to his brothers' scientific success. This was a key factor in obtaining his personal commitment to having the federal government assume the main financial responsibility for promoting pure research in leading-edge areas of medicine, science and engineering and technology. Chrétien seemed sensitive to the fact that he hadn't emulated his siblings, to the same degree and depth, in his own education and training. He would suggest, however, that despite his lack of formal training in economics and finance, he had effectively dispelled their mysteries in very practical ways through his repeated encounters with the top federal government bureaucrats and economic advisers, from his earliest days as parliamentary secretary to Mitchell Sharp, onwards.

There are occasional remarks in Chrétien's memoirs that indicate a continuing concern with the issue, nevertheless. Thus did he sum up Mark MacGuigan as "too educated for his intelligence; he seemed to stumble over his degrees, and that hurt him as a politician." MacGuigan had come to the House of Commons with a double doctorate (in Philosophy from Toronto, and in Legal Science from Columbia), and had served on the law faculties of Toronto and York universities and as law dean at Windsor. A Liberal MP for twelve years, he had not been able to advance beyond the rank of parliamentary secretary in the Trudeau government before finally achieving the foreign ministry in 1980, and then the justice ministry in 1982.[102] Even though he had been no more than a longshot leadership candidate at the 1984 convention, MacGuigan was dropped by the eventual winner and prime-minister-to-be, John Turner, from his advance cabinet list. Instead, the outgoing prime minister, Pierre Trudeau, named him to the Federal Court of Canada.

Advanced education can sometimes be a restraining factor if one delays too long in trying to see every possible side of any question. Sometimes the most innovatory members of a government will be those, without the burden of too much formal training, who can grasp the nettle in timely fashion. In the first Chrétien mandate, only three of the new cabinet ministers lacked a post-secondary degree. One of these was Fisheries Minister Brian Tobin. At Tobin's direct request, I had once explained to him, at short notice and in a brief quarter hour before he went into the House, the then recently signed United Nations Third Convention on the Law of the Sea, which had been twelve years in the making. Tobin,

---

[102] MacGuigan, as a cabinet minister, proved to be unusually cautious in advancing his own considered ideas, in view of his unusual claims to expertise. His interrupted academic and then his subsequent political careers may not therefore have attained their full potential. Some of his colleagues, including Ron Irwin, who was his parliamentary secretary, felt that, as a neophyte in the foreign affairs portfolio, he had been too deferential to President Reagan's first secretary of state, General Alexander Haig, whom Reagan was later to discard because of Haig's occasional obvious errors in political judgement.

as fisheries minister, was concerned with the treaty's implications for the pending legal suit by Spain and Portugal over Canada's actions to prevent their illegal over-fishing of vanishing turbot stocks off our Atlantic coast. Tobin had no difficulty at all in seizing the issues from this corridor briefing and running with them.[103]

Chrétien's judgement that one doesn't have to be an economist to comprehend difficult financial problems provided one is prepared to take expert advice, and has the ability to choose one's expert advisers well, is obviously correct. At the same time, a certain discomfort in relation to the accepted Quebec francophone intellectual establishment of the day seems present in Chrétien's dismissal of *Le Devoir's* politically influential, longtime editor-in-chief, Claude Ryan, as "a little bit pompous . . . you feel you are in front of a bishop. You almost have to put your knee on the floor and kiss his ring." Chrétien gave strong advice to Ryan not to seek the Quebec provincial Liberal leadership and not to run for public office. "Your talent is to be the editor of *Le Devoir*," he told Ryan.

Throughout his tenure at *Le Devoir*, Ryan maintained — usually on late Monday evenings after completion of his day's work and in his second floor editorial offices in an antique building at 211 rue du Saint-Sacrement in the Old Town — an informal seminar of leading Quebec thinkers to discuss the main socio-economic and constitutional issues affecting Quebec and Canada. The invited participants, who cheerfully came along, sometimes included Pierre Trudeau (before his election to Parliament). There was no question as to Ryan's ease of communication in the give-and-take

---

[103] I had told Tobin that international law, in high political issues like the dispute with Spain and Portugal, is fifty percent old legal rules and fifty percent the sheer poetry of re-interpreting these rules, imaginatively, in a contemporary context. Tobin replied that since he was a Newfoundlander, he could supply the poetry, and of course he did. His ministry had recovered an illegal Spanish fishing net from the Atlantic, and Tobin had it hung up on a barge in the East River, right outside the UN building in New York. He then went on to win his case in the International Court in The Hague, on a technical-legal point to be sure, but he had already won it in the public relations arena.

of the discussions, or his skill in analyzing and synthesizing the different points of view. Ryan went on, of course, to become leader of the Quebec Liberal party, Member of the Quebec National Assembly and leader of the opposition in Quebec, and afterwards a senior minister in the third Bourassa government in 1985. Whether Ryan had the extra elements — the "royal jelly" as Donald Macdonald called it — to become premier of Quebec must remain open since Ryan fell short in his one and only opportunity against Premier René Lévesque in 1981. But the empirical record suggests that the gap between capacity for large ideas and capacity to be elected can be bridged, if the will to learn is there.

Jean Chrétien's constitutional style as prime minister produced an accentuation of the "presidentialization" of the office already manifested significantly in the preceding Trudeau and Mulroney governments. Chrétien, like Trudeau and Mulroney, had much too large a cabinet. He had begun office in 1993 with a determined reduction in the number of full ministers. But he soon returned to the bad old ways and had increased cabinet numbers by the end of 2000 to the inflated levels achieved by his two immediate predecessors.[104] And, of course, Chrétien had no designated or recognized inner cabinet in which genuinely collegial decision-making could operate. As noted earlier, this meant that while the prime minister might choose to delegate fully those highly technical, functional areas such as finance and science and industry, which were outside the prime minister's own professional training, experience and competence (or his continuing interest), he would try to maintain a full monitoring of the rest of his ministers, at least with regard to the larger policy issues inherent in their mandates.

This was especially noticeable with foreign affairs, as it had been under Trudeau and Mulroney before him. The current *"mondialization"* of so many erstwhile primarily domestic issues in industry

---

[104] The Turner and Campbell interim prime-ministerships have been regarded, as they must, as incidental for the purposes of the major discussions in this text.

and trade and commerce, as well as the overall impact in the post-
Cold War period of defence and security issues on internal policies,
made it more or less inevitable that the prime minister involve
himself fully with the macro-policy issues of foreign affairs.[105] An
expansion in numbers and a strengthening in expertise and *de
facto* authority of the prime minister's personal secretariat would
flow logically from this.

Prime Minister Chrétien has ventured some interesting comparisons between two of his predecessors, Trudeau and Pearson,
and their personal styles as prime minister. He refuted what he
called a common assumption today that Pearson ran a chaotic
administration, with a certain benign weakness and lack of direction. On the contrary, he suggested that Pearson was "very, very
tough in managing his ministers," even while facing the "normal
difficulties of minority governments, compounded by a Leader of
the Opposition who was highly irresponsible." Chrétien here
meant John Diefenbaker. As Chrétien concluded in *Straight from
the Heart:* "He [Pearson] had his own ideas, and most of the time
he just did what he wanted to do." The picture painted by Chrétien is one that, drawing on Pearson's very early university teaching
career, corresponds more or less exactly to a rather authoritarian
college dean who, under the gentle façade of allowing interminable faculty discussions without conclusion, ends up making
the decisions himself, in default. "His cheery awkwardness made
everyone want to come to his rescue, and there was a lot of warmth
for him that didn't exist for Trudeau later."

Chrétien's conclusion, nevertheless, was that in the end Trudeau
proved much more consensus-oriented in his approach to government decision-making than Pearson. He attributed this situation
in considerable part to the experience of Trudeau's second (minority) government, 1972–1974, when Trudeau was dependent on
the support of the NDP and thus compelled to deal with the NDP's

---

[105] Even as early as the First World War, when the British government insti-
tuted its first inner war cabinet, the foreign affairs minister was deliberately
excluded from the designated five-members on the grounds that the prime
minister could and should handle any such issues himself.

brilliantly articulate leader, David Lewis. This caused Trudeau to learn, by trial-and-error, the necessary flexibility and ability to compromise in order to survive, and to build *ad hoc* a majority vote in the House of Commons on key issues of the government's program. One might add, however, that Trudeau's range of engaged intellectual interest tended to be limited to those few subjects on which, from his early studies and travel, he had both expert knowledge and also strong opinions — federalism and the constitution to be sure, and also foreign policy. On most other matters, Trudeau could afford to adopt a college seminar approach and leave it to his cabinet or even his national caucus to arrive at any consensus before deciding himself to act.

A similar conclusion seems correct with Prime Minister Chrétien: that he is selective, even casually selective, in his own *direct* engagement in policy issues. Priority interests have remained, of course. Macro-constitutional issues have been a special concern and interest for him ever since Trudeau recruited him as his chief political lieutenant in the constitutional patriation project. To this we must add aboriginal affairs and Native land treaties (from Chrétien's ministerial portfolio, three decades earlier, 1968–1974, to which he had given his own most creative thought, and in the end, in vain). In foreign policy, he has focused at least on Canada-US relations and G-8 questions. However, even on these priority concerns, he often chose the "tough cop/kind cop" game of letting someone else assume the responsibility and political blame for an unpleasant or unpopular governmental policy, so that he himself could then emerge as the "nice guy always ready with a compromise."[106]

This characterization would apply to the federal government's constitutional strategy after the national near-disaster in the second Quebec sovereignty-association referendum of October 1995. The new federal minister of intergovernmental affairs, Stéphane

---

[106] Chrétien has ascribed just such role-playing to the federal constitutional team in 1980–1982, with his colleague John Roberts being cast as the "arrogant" federal player and Chrétien himself appearing, happily, as the pleasant consensus builder.

Dion, was reduced as a francophone from Quebec to saying NO! to Quebec, and to attacking Quebec nationalists in the House. The wise, elder statesman, francophone prime minister, on the other hand, could afford gestures of federal self-restraint, and pragmatic intergovernmental accommodation. However, after all the fascinating if ultimately failed, federal paradigms and models for a new, or at least renewed, Canadian federalism left over from the Trudeau and Mulroney eras, one still has no impression of any interesting new thinking at the federal level after the 1993 election. There is, as has already been observed a number of times, no real sense of any movement on the constitutional reform front. At the core of this malaise is also the issue of executive-legislative relations, as the key to a recasting of the constitutional role of Parliament and of the MPs within it so that, in the popular phrase, the MPs may finally have "something useful to do."

The absence of scope thinking, Trudeau-style, on the goals of the new, plural Canadian society of today, and on the best ways of achieving those goals, seems to be a result, in some measure, of weaknesses at the executive level. This has resulted from an inability to recruit the best possible executive talent under the present constitutional system, which links entry into the federal cabinet and government to election to Parliament — a rather different arena, requiring rather different talents to those needed for executive government. The failure to open up federal decision-making opportunities to the new talent graduating from Canadian universities and professional schools has itself been a powerful impulse for the "brain drain" to the financially far more ample opportunities and challenges in the United States. This is a condition accentuated by the new continentalism and the removal under Canada-US free-trade agreements of the clogs, legal and other, formerly existing on the free flow of goods and services and professional people across the common frontier. These new factors, much more than the traditional constitutional demands from Quebec, provide the more significant questions today as to the future of Canadian federalism.

Legacy Quest

Timing, as President Franklin Roosevelt used to say, is the key in politics. When Chrétien first campaigned, as a new leader of the opposition in the 1993 general election, it had not been expected that a Liberal majority government would result. I and other new party candidates were advised to keep our constituency campaign organizations active and ready — even to hold on to our campaign signs — to prepare for the eventuality of a minority Liberal government, which would be followed by an early, snap election call in order to produce a full majority — much on the earlier scenario of John Diefenbaker's leap from a minority government status after the 1957 election to a then record majority in the ensuing 1958 election.

This was not to be in 1993. The Conservatives, after Prime Minister Mulroney's resignation, went into the elections with a new, untried but apparently exciting young leader, and with a comfortable lead in the polls which lasted well into the actual campaign. Then, in the last two weeks of the campaign, they saw it all vanish disastrously, as they were swept away. Forming a new majority government after the October 1993 victory, and faced by a weak and divided opposition of four small, mutually incompatible parties, the new prime minister saw no need to mount any ambitious new legislative program. This reinforced his sense that voters were worn out after all the excitement of the Trudeau and Mulroney administrations and wanted a period of calm and rest and, above all, an end to the great constitutional debate over Quebec. There had been, to be sure, the Liberal party "Red Book" of campaign promises, but these sorts of electoral platforms tended to be viewed with public cynicism. Certainly, this had been so since Trudeau had campaigned successfully in 1974 against Conservative Robert Stanfield's proposals for wage and price control, then promptly introduced them himself after his re-election. The Red Book promise to abolish the much hated goods and services tax (GST) that had been introduced by the Mulroney government as a happy new

revenue source, was ignored. Only maverick Liberal MP and former Liberal opposition "rat pack" member, John Nunziata, who
had been left out of the new cabinet, and that other former Liberal
"rat packer," Sheila Copps, who had made it into the new cabinet,
seemed to feel twinges of public conscience about this. Whereas
insistence upon implementing the Red Book promise would drive
Nunziata out of the Liberal caucus altogether, the government's
failure to do so would cause Sheila Copps quixotically to resign her
seat as an MP, only to run again and win in a by-election before
being restored to cabinet. My feeling is that it might have been better for Chrétien's ultimate performance as prime minister, and
thus his ultimate place in history, if he had been elected in 1993
with only a minority government. This would have provided the
political stimulus to spell out a "one-hundred-days-of-achievement"
operational program in the run-up to new elections. Almost certainly, it would have propelled him to choose his new cabinet with
some more obvious concern for professional qualifications and
experience rather than past personal loyalties.

One never did hear any satisfying constitutional-legal explanation of the necessity for an early dissolution of Parliament in June
1997, only three-and-a-half years into the Chrétien government's
first term in office, and without any defeat in the House or national crisis demanding it. The only credible explanation ventured at
the time was that some people did not like fall elections because
they spoiled the preceding summer holidays. The dissension between the opposition parties was clearly no mere temporary, passing condition, and would surely remain the same, if not worsen,
with the passage of time.

If Jean Chrétien had decided some time around 1998 that his
best legacy would be as the Canadian prime minister who succeeded in balancing the federal budget again after all those bad
years of deficit spending under two powerful prime ministers,
Trudeau and Mulroney, and if he had then presided gracefully
over a transition in power to some favoured successor within the
party, he would have departed with full honours in an atmosphere
of general affection and respect. At certain moments during his

first mandate, he had even hinted at just such a preference for two terms — for personal, family reasons. His decision to stay on and run for a third appears to have been influenced in part by his anger, and even more perhaps by the outrage of his family and his PMO palace guard, at what was viewed as a premature campaign for the succession to the party leadership and thus the prime-ministership on the part of would-be dauphins within caucus. It has been observed before that Chrétien is a stubborn and proud man, and that if you try to push him in a certain direction, he will usually respond by doing just the opposite.

I am also persuaded that there was another, more romantic factor in his decision to seek a third successive electoral victory as PM: the desire to leave behind some special legacy of his own — a personal contribution to history. It is curious that so many political leaders leave the making of their legacies until the obvious twilight years of their public careers. Trudeau, for example, waited until his fourth term in office (1980–1984) to unveil both his constitutional patriation package and his new "third force" foreign policy. Chrétien, in the informal luncheons at 24 Sussex Drive with some of his MPs, had been reminded, halfway into his second mandate, that with the departures of Chancellor Kohl of Germany and President Mitterand of France, and the impending end of US President Clinton's second term, he would — if he continued in office beyond January 2001 — be senior serving head-of-government among the G-8 leaders. With memories of his successful 1993 campaign metaphor about the experienced older helmsman who steers the ship safely into port during the storm, he was clearly impressed by that new fact.

He, of course, sensibly would have to develop some new programs and new ideas. And he certainly would need some new faces in a visibly tiring cabinet that had lost the energy and excitement from the victory over the Mulroney/Campbell Conservatives all those years earlier. Or so one would have thought. Chrétien, however, had always prided himself, publicly, on the fact that his was a scandal-free government, and that he had never been forced to dismiss a minister for misconduct in office. The negative side of that boast was that, with his own deep reluctance to let anyone go from his original group of loyal supporters, he had experienced no occasion for ministerial change or for bringing new blood and new ideas into the cabinet. Consequently, he went into the late-2000 electoral campaign with virtually the same old team, and without any new programs. He won again: indeed, with a slightly increased majority. But his victory was tarnished by the dismally low voter turnout — which seemed attributable to the continued weakness and mutual intransigence (worse than before) of the four opposition parties.

Then, although this had not been generally foreseen or predicted in Ottawa before the elections, it was suddenly all downhill. Internal contradictions within the federal Liberal party rose to the fore (among them, the bicephalic leadership structure of party organization and parliamentary caucus). Long-term historical forces already in motion during the Trudeau and Mulroney administrations (notably the special Canada-US bilateral relationship that had been further consolidated and strengthened in financial and economic terms with the two free-trade agreements) took on crisis aspects. And the Chrétien government was caught in the middle. The minor Shakespearian tragedy that ensued in Ottawa might have been avoided on Chrétien's part by an earlier, timely departure of his own choosing and on his own terms, leaving his successor to resolve the contradictions and the crises. The inevitable conflicts might have been countered or at least mitigated in their more pathological aspects, but that would have required a rather different cast of characters in Ottawa and a rather different intellectual milieu in which to make the key governmental decisions.

"Lame Duck" Factor

In August 2002, only a year and a half after his third successive majority electoral victory, with the extra premium of a slight increase in the Liberal majority in the House of Commons, Prime

Minister Chrétien announced that he would quit his post before the next federal general election. Claude Ryan commented acerbically in the 22 August 2002 edition of *Le Devoir* that the prime minister had chosen a way of leaving that was strewn with misunderstandings, evasions, intrigues and calculated self-interest. Ryan concluded that the prime minister's departure had become in the preceding months a necessity from which he could not escape. While Chrétien multiplied his travels abroad, two factors, in Ryan's opinion, had undermined his leadership inside Canada: the stories of political patronage awarded in Quebec, and an excessive animosity to Paul Martin.

The patronage "scandal" was certainly the first public break in the honeymoon relationship, normally accorded for a few months only by the media to any newly elected leader, but which in Chrétien's case had endured through three elections. This so-called scandal centered on a number of ministers who had been personally close to the PM, and who, generally, were considered as having been put in cabinet for that reason alone. Most of them were from Quebec. The term "corruption" was frequently used by the press, I think inaccurately, for there was never any evidentiary basis for suggesting personal financial gain or profit for the ministers concerned. The adverse public reaction stemmed, rather, from a sea change in public attitudes in very recent years to how the political processes should operate and what the role of an elected MP should be in the dispensing of public monies and public contracts.

In defending embattled ministers against charges that they had accepted benefits from corporations or persons seeking government grants or contracts, or that they had awarded such grants or contracts to relatives or friends or financial donors to the party, the suggestion was made by government spokespersons that the ministers who, of course, under the British parliamentary executive system are also MPs, were acting no differently than ordinary MPs. What wasn't perceived was that the electorate had matured to the point where this type of conduct was now unacceptable equally for cabinet ministers and for ordinary MPs. The "old" and earlier-tolerated political custom of rewards for friends of the party in power was simply out-of-date. Claude Ryan, when he became leader of the Quebec provincial Liberals, established rigorous standards of moral and financial advance screening for all would-be candidates for his party that would effectively place them, like Caesar's wife, above suspicion. Ryan was well in advance of his time, in this respect, in Quebec and in Canada generally. But his reforms, however initially unpopular, were there to stay and can be credited, I think, with initiating the change in general thinking throughout Canada on the need to eliminate patronage practices.[107]

Within the space of a few short months in 2002, a prime minister who had prided himself on the probity of his cabinet, suddenly found himself compelled to accept ministerial resignations under fire, to shuffle other ministers to lesser posts, and, generally, to defend day-after-day in the House the half a dozen ministers (some from Quebec, but as many from the English-speaking provinces), who, in the view of a newly vigilant Ottawa-based media, had offended against the new standards of public office. It was sad for the prime minister, and sad for the ministers concerned, who, according to their own views, had done nothing contrary to the well-established ground rules of Ottawa behaviour. Part of the media irritation was certainly created by the previously discussed, ineffectual ministerial ethics system then in place.

The PM, after the latest in the series of such political disasters in 2002, announced plans to accelerate the creation of a new ethics system, with an independent federal ethics commissioner who would now oversee all MPs, whether ministers or not. But the dramatic sea change in public opinion and public expectations as to the proper standards of behaviour in public office might prove more than enough, in itself, to ensure severe electoral sanctions against deemed incompetents or delinquents in office, or against governments that put them there.

---

[107] In Ryan's own case, however, these reforms may have hastened his replacement by Robert Bourassa as Quebec Liberal party chief and leader of the opposition, particularly when combined with his loss to Premier Lévesque in the 1981 Quebec elections.

More poignant for the Prime Minister, perhaps, was the civil war within the federal Liberal party organization outside Parliament. The party bureaucracy had traditionally supported the incumbent party leader who, after all, was selected according to the party constitution by delegates elected for that purpose from all the constituencies in the country. It was the party bureaucracy, centralized in Ottawa, that controlled the party finances, most of which had been raised by the PM's annual or biannual public dinners held across the country. Chrétien's personal loyalists within the party organization were unpleasantly surprised to find that they had lost effective control, and that they were being voted out of office even at the time of Chrétien's successful third election campaign in November 2000. These incumbents had grown too comfortable in office and had neglected working contact with the grass-roots membership.[108]

What produced the federal Liberal internal crisis by mid-2002 were the fruits of the party's constitutional dualism of party organization and parliamentary caucus created, all those years ago by Mackenzie King for no better reason, apparently, than his belief in the advantages of the extra electoral propaganda and public relations windfall to be achieved by aping the quadrennial conventions of the two major US political parties. It is not clear from the succession to party leadership and thus to parliamentary caucus leadership in the history of the federal Liberal party since Mackenzie King's election in 1919, that the results would have been

---

[108] In my own constituency association of Vancouver Quadra, a very able, hard-working, and ethnoculturally representative executive had been obliged to work hard to resist a take-over in 1999 by student activists and others already working on behalf of a Paul Martin bid for the party leadership. I saw no problem in this sort of challenge, as such. The existing Quadra constituency executive had fought back and won. I met with the challengers after they had lost to discuss their concerns. They were disturbed at what they thought was an absence of any serious policy debate within the parliamentary party, and at what they characterized as a politic of drifting along with the current. They wanted to get the party and the country moving again. I saw the danger signals, but it was difficult to get the message received and understood and acted upon in Ottawa.

any different if the choice had been that of the elected MPs in the parliamentary caucus rather than of a party convention called for the purpose. The examples are only six in number: King, St. Laurent, Pearson, Trudeau, Turner and Chrétien. But the way was opened constitutionally those many years ago to designation or deposition of an incumbent prime minister through the extra-parliamentary instrument of a party convention vote called by an extra-parliamentary institution, the party organization.

It was this constitutional-legal fact and the political facts of life, which by mid-2002 were of general public knowledge, that may have been the final factor impelling Prime Minister Chrétien to announce publicly in August 2002 that he would resign. The equivocations that Claude Ryan had signalled in his commentary in *Le Devoir*, namely the separation of the promise to resign from the actual timing of its taking effect, reflected the give-and-take between rival factions within the party. It also involved the recognition by the main contender for the succession, at least, that concession to political courtesies and the etiquette of political face-saving in allowing as graceful a parting as possible would be wise, if sufficient party internal consensus and goodwill were to be maintained so as to win any ensuing general elections.

The parliamentary caucus, throughout these events, always remained the potential key player in the final outcome. In the end, the office of prime minister is still determined by his or her ability to maintain majority support within the House of Commons, either (and preferably) within his or her own party alone, or else in coalition with, or with firm guarantees of support from a sufficiency of MPs on the opposition side of the House to produce and maintain a voting majority in the House on budgetary and other key issues. While the governor general might properly choose to take judicial notice of facts of general public knowledge and thus of the existence and effective power of extra-parliamentary bodies like the party organization, the governor general must always yield, constitutionally, to a prime minister controlling, by whatever combination of MPs, a majority in the House.

In the special circumstances of August 2002, there was never any doubt about what the Ottawa media characterized as an attempted *coup d'état* within the federal Liberal party. In spite of a counterattack by Chrétien loyalists within the cabinet, the results, as communicated by the regional caucus chairs within the overall national caucus, were clear and unequivocal. There simply were not enough votes to counter the preponderant power of the challenger or challengers established within the party organization. There were just too many rank-and-file MPs frustrated by the perceived absence of opportunity for promotion within the government, and by the prime minister's continued maintenance in office of ministers deemed by the fractious MPs to have no particular skills and to have long since run out of ideas. The cadre of core loyalists among the ministers certainly exercised effective control over the disciplinary posts of government whip and government House Leader (with their potentially arbitrary or capricious powers over the caucus). But when the political crunch came, they were unable to deliver the necessary guaranteed support for the leader. Chrétien's most spirited and moving defence seemed to come from relatively junior people like Martin Cauchon and Denis Coderre from Quebec. In contrast, some of the more marginal people among ministers, secretaries of state and MPs who owed everything to the PM for having directly appointed them party candidates without their having to run the gauntlet of a contested nomination, maintained a deafening silence.

The sort of temporary, military truce fashioned between the rival forces within the party to carry over a now seemingly inevitable, brokered transition in leadership would be unique in Canadian constitutionalism in its agreed duration, eighteen months,[109] and also in its failure to spell out the consequences, in terms of interim decision-making power within the government. There

---

[109] One should note that Louis St. Laurent was elected leader of the federal Liberal party on 7 August 1948, but did not become prime minister until Mackenzie King left office on 15 November that year.

would be certain risks in this, and the answers would probably only come with some trial-and-error testing. In strict constitutional-legal terms, however, all the discretionary prerogative powers inherent in the office of prime minister would and should constitutionally remain with the incumbent until he gave it up — as agreed, in advance, in February 2004. The governor general, as titular head-of-state, would deal properly with that as a constitutional "given," as would foreign governments and their representatives. The only constitutional-legal limitation would come from the prime minister's own sense of self-restraint and the political limits to the exercise of his office in what might be called a political "lame-duck" period. Such considerations, one might note, have not proved particularly constraining on United States presidents in the interregnum between a Presidential election on the first Tuesday of November and the inauguration of a successor, especially a successor from a different party, on 20 January the following year.

And there is no reason, in constitutional law, why they should constrain Prime Minister Chrétien in this most recent experiment with a Canadian interregnum. Order-in-council appointments made during the interregnum period could, save for judicial appointments which are protected under existing constitutional principles, always be revoked by the order-in-council decrees of any successor, although this would be an unusual step that would be unlikely to be attempted. This situation is distinguishable from the experience with order-in-council appointments, and especially controversial diplomatic appointments left unsigned from the Trudeau and the short-lived Turner administrations, which a successor prime minister of a different party refused to approve in 1984.

In summation, the brokered transition arrangements as to party leadership, with the unduly long time span in the ensuing interregnum, may raise more constitutional contradictions and practical inconveniences than the temporary political benefits thought to be conferred. One wonders whether it might not be sensible and timely to consider, in any future constitutional reexamination and revision, dropping the hybrid British and American process now used by the federal Liberal party (and some other federal and provincial political parties) to choose a leader. The object would be to return the power to choose the party leader to the parliamentary caucus in the House of Commons.[110]

Prime Minister Chrétien, in any case, acted correctly in constitutional-legal terms in maintaining his own prerogatives. The prime minister's decision in the aftermath of the 11 September 2001 terrorist attacks to name a strong deputy prime minister, John Manley, to have overall charge of all security related arrangements in the government, was a bold initiative, with immediate and observable, concrete improvements in federal government operations. One wondered why Prime Minister Chrétien had not done it before. He had often seemed not to be too interested in the details of administration, or in providing a continuing oversight and coordination of the different ministries.

The Manley appointment, which some compared favourably to Vice President Cheney's "prime-ministerial" role in President George W. Bush's administration, supplied a coherence and cohesiveness in overall government policy-making that had been noticeably lacking before. The effective delegation, for the first time, of the day-to-day running of the government to a strong, deliberately non-flamboyant deputy prime minister — much as Nehru had done with Patel, in the early years of the post-independence federal state of India — would leave Chrétien free to pursue those larger G-8 interests in which he seemed to feel his larger legacy would be formed.

It was also at this time that the embattled prime minister made

---

[110] One may wish also to note the corollary power of a parliamentary caucus to depose a sitting prime minister. For example, three-term prime minister, Margaret Thatcher (1979–1990) — the longest serving PM in twentieth-century Britain — was shown the door by her Conservative caucus. In Australia, four-term prime minister, Bob Hawke (1983–1991), was voted out by his Labor party caucus.

some long overdue cabinet appointments, albeit as replacements for long-serving ministers who had quit under fire. Several of those appointed had been first elected in the bright new class of 1993. Unfortunately, some of their early intellectual energy and fresh ideas clearly had been dissipated over the years of enforced idleness on the back benches. Bill Graham was brought in to replace John Manley as foreign minister. Wayne Easter was given one of the recognized "disaster" posts in the cabinet as solicitor general after the incumbent, Lawrence MacAulay, had to be given his leave precipitately. Marlene Catterall who, as parliamentary assistant to the government House Leader, had done much to raise quality in the performance in question period on the government side, was finally promoted to government whip. I thought the PM missed an opportunity to make a really imaginative choice for the conveniently vacated defence portfolio by reaching outside Parliament for someone with acknowledged military-strategic status and expertise. This would have been excellent for the morale of the armed forces to have, for the first time in many years, someone who had had direct military service and preferably actual combat experience. Such a person might better understand their needs and also the limits of their operational capacities, given the dangerously diminished state of defence spending in the federal budgets of recent years. It was not to be, however.

The building of a legacy, for someone charged with running a government, is better begun from the very outset of one's term of office, and not left as a historical footnote to one's twilight days, when the rapidly diminishing time capital becomes controlling. In this connection, one thinks of President Franklin Roosevelt in November 1932, after his election victory, promising "One Hundred Days" of action to conquer the impact of the world economic depression in the United States. The immediate result may have been much trial and error experimentation, but it set the intellectual tone for the subsequent four-term Roosevelt era.

VII

~m~

CONSTITUTIONAL
POSTSCRIPT

The Long Farewell

I had told Jean Chrétien in the spring of 1992, when I accepted his invitation to become a candidate, that, if nominated and then elected, I would plan to serve one full term, and that I would re-examine toward the end of that Parliament whether to run for re-election. In fact, I had yet to consider the question when the prime minister called his snap, early election for June 1997. He asked me to stand for re-election. His first term, after almost three decades of deficit financing, had been preoccupied, understandably enough, with balancing the federal budget to the effective exclusion of most other long-range policy challenges. However, with the target date for a balanced budget approaching, there would be time in a second mandate for other things of concern to my constituents and myself. I accepted the challenge.[111] Then it was back to Ottawa with an agenda for change. When, to my surprise, at the beginning of October 2000, Prime Minister Chrétien announced yet another early election, I told him that I would not be seeking a third term.

My farewell courtesy call on the prime minister at his 24 Sussex Drive residence, which I had expected to last about fifteen minutes, extended to well over two hours, and ended only then because Brian Tobin arrived from Newfoundland (on a trip made especially to discuss his own renewed federal candidacy). The PM asked me if I would consider continuing to serve in another capacity, mentioning a high, prerogative post that was soon to become vacant. I, however, thought that this, in its particular timing, might send a wrong constitutional message. I was reminded of the lines from Robert Browning's "The Lost Leader": "Just for a handful of silver he left us, / Just for a riband to stick on his coat." I was not planning an early retirement, but simply a lateral move to return, for a period of years at least, to my earlier mode of engagement in public affairs, national and international, as a scholar and writer and adviser.

The prime minister ranged widely over his own achievements and disappointments in office, and what he thought he might leave by way of historical legacy. He talked about his aspirations nearly forty years before on first entering federal politics. I mentioned that I had visited his childhood home in Shawinigan and talked to some surviving neighbours, a fact that he particularly appreciated — for this provided an opportunity to discuss his rural Quebec roots, and the historical division between the original small anglophone social and commercial elite and the larger francophone workforce. Chrétien reminisced (as he had done on several earlier occasions) that as a child he had often walked by the splendid local golf course, which had been built in the style of clas-

---

[111] Alan Beesley and Dave Pasin headed my new campaign team (this time, with Ana-Maria Hobrough as the candidate's aide). We again won easily, this time with the highest percentage for a winning Liberal candidate west of Winnipeg.

sical Scottish links, but which did not have any francophone members. Something of the clash in his own soul between the innate conservatism of his Quebec family background and his sense of the injustice or unfairness of the social processes comes out in anecdotes such as these and explains the frequent ambivalence in his approach to policy-making and policy choices in later life. For example, he had supported to the full, and perhaps beyond, his first finance minister, Paul Martin, in his fiscal integrity program and the drive for a balanced federal budget after almost three decades of deficits, but once this goal was finally attained in 1998 he inclined easily enough toward the social welfare elements in the Liberal party thinking. His effective killing of the second serious attempt at a merger between two of the five trading banks in November 2002, after the failure of the much more ambitious attempts at merger in 1998, may have reflected as much the left-wing liberal aversion to concentration of great power in too few hands, as any cool, in-depth study of the economic issues at play, or their continentalist rationale.

In historical terms, Chrétien's decade or so of service as prime minister straddles a period of transition and fundamental change in Canadian society: from biculturalism as political fact-of-life and constitutional basic premise, to multiculturalism, and then on to social pluralism as the erstwhile cultural-linguistic frontiers and barriers between the different communities, old (founding) and recent, give way to the new Canadian community of communities. Chrétien inherited Canada's open-door immigration policies from both Trudeau and Mulroney. The new continentalism and the resultant economic and emerging political integration with the United States were largely a legacy from Mulroney, who had signed the free-trade agreements with the US. What these earlier actors had not foreseen, however, was the rapidity with which the new policy initiatives would become concretized, socially as well as legally. The events simply galloped along, often unaffected by the attempts of the latter-day actors to control or effectively influence their unfolding.

Is a prime minister in an era of historical transition doomed to be a transitional figure himself? One speaks of John XXIII (1958–1963) as a "Pope of transition" in a laudatory sense. Because he knew (given his age on election — seventy-seven — and his poor health) that he had but a short span of years in office, he set out to revolutionize an atrophied system to give it a conscious, purposive direction, and to remain master of the events. But John XXIII took office not too long after the cataclysmic events of World War II, and at the time of the mounting criticisms of his aristocratic, austere and aloof predecessor, Pius XII. The time was ripe, historically, for a more down-to-earth personality with populist impulses. Jean Chrétien hardly inherited such a favourable opportunity for fundamental change in 1993. He was, I think, completely correct in his reading that the country was not interested, at least for the time being, in any more great debates on the constitution or constitutional-governmental change, after the heated battles of the 1980s and early 1990s and the spectacular failures of Meech Lake and Charlottetown. The financial exigencies of the early 1990s, and the inherited record federal deficit budget of $42.8 billion for 1992–1993, appeared more than enough in themselves to inhibit him from large-scale, imaginative new ventures in social policy-making.

For some of the problems for which he has been severely criticized in recent times — the "presidentialization" of the office of prime minister, and the corresponding downgrading, devaluation and effective diminution of the role of Parliament, MPs and cabinet ministers, too — he was not himself present at the creation. These basic conditions went back through the Mulroney administration to the earliest Trudeau years and, in any case, have proved endemic to the Westminster-style parliamentary executive wherever it has been exported or "received" in constitutional form. Some might even suggest, in fact, that Chrétien's presidential palace guard, though able, was too limited in numbers and in range of expertise and given mandate to handle the new policy-making demands with full effectiveness. This was, perhaps, most noticeable in the realm of foreign policy. The prime minister, like most of his peer group from other leading industrial countries, was most often called on to assume the honorific, public aspects once formerly assumed by the titular head of state (governor general) or delegated to the foreign minister. The prime minister had some very able young staffers on loan from diplomatic service in the PMO, but none of them with the political stature and authority or acquired practical wisdom of Eddie Goldenberg or Jean Pelletier. Hence, the occasional, embarrassing public gaffes or contradictions concerning relations with the United States or the Middle East.

The "new politics" involved the demand for squeaky-clean MPs and ministers, who would never dispense financial favours or hand out contracts and grants to party supporters or personal friends and relatives. The new "people's power" involved action in the streets, public demonstrations, mass write-in and e-mail campaigns, as a protest against diverse issues and organizations like the proposed MAI (Multilateral Agreement of Investment) program or the WTO (World Trade Organization) or the biennial summit meetings of the APEC (Asia-Pacific Economic Cooperation Forum) heads-of-state, or even against government *per se*. Then there was the growing call for an end to the "patronage" system in promotions or appointments to federal government positions. All these trends were there and apparent before Chrétien entered office as prime minister. For example, in many respects the intellectual call-to-arms for the new "people's power" had its roots in Pierre Trudeau's advocacy, years earlier, of "participatory democracy." For Jean Chrétien, entering Parliament in his twenties under the "old politics" and in a governmental system accustomed to it, the question must be whether he could or should have done more to contain or alter it (as Claude Ryan had tried, with only partial success, to do in Quebec in the late 1970s and early 1980s).

Harry Truman was a leader whom Chrétien had admired from a historical distance, and in many respects considered as a model of someone who, without very many educational or financial opportunities in his early life, but with strong family values and equally strong populist impulses, had gone on to become one of the really great US Presidents. Truman was much criticized during his presidency for being a product of the "old politics," and for tolerating practices of "cronyism" and political "influence" in public decisions. But Truman's absolute personal integrity was never in doubt, and these particular criticisms soon yielded to the larger valuation of his courage and realism in foreign policy decisions and his ability to assemble and build a professional team within his administration. On Chrétien's personal integrity, I have never had any doubt, and the judgement of history will surely be the same.

Certainly, I also well understood Chrétien's loyalty to those who had worked for him in his several bids to gain the party leadership. As indicated elsewhere, I thought he stayed too long with some of them as members of his cabinet, especially after their abilities to measure up to the job were seriously in question. At the latest, once he had made the personal decision — presumably in 1998 — to soldier on for a further, third mandate or beyond that, to even a fourth mandate, he should have begun to clean house in the certain knowledge that any debts of personal loyalty had long since been paid off. A new team would have meant an opening to new ideas and new policies to develop programs to take the country into the early years of the new century — something clearly essential if one were to meet a new public restlessness. In the words so successfully employed by presidential candidate John F. Kennedy in 1960, Chrétien needed to "get the country moving again."

The elements of a Shakespearian-style minor tragedy are there, nevertheless, in the manner and circumstances of the transition now underway in the federal Liberal party leadership. It was noticeable that some of those whom the prime minister had retained as cabinet ministers (or in similar prestige or power posts), notwithstanding their indiscretions or blunders in office, not only didn't support him when he was under attack, but even came out against him in public with calls for his early resignation and departure from office. Chrétien might have meditated, like Cardinal

Wolsey in his long farewell to all his former greatness, upon their ingratitude, but instead proceeded with his own personal agenda for history, apparently not fully grasping that he would be judged, finally, on the empirical record of his decade in office as prime minister and his slightly longer term as party leader. The earliest and best images are of Chrétien as Walt Whitman's "Happy Warrior," a leader who genuinely enjoyed the give-and-take of exchanges in the House and who mastered, more than his predecessors, the challenge of organizing and winning successive national electoral campaigns.

His reputation in history also would be determined, in considerable measure, by the record of his successors in office in mastering the long-range historical forces already there when Chrétien had first gained office in 1993. If the intraparty succession struggle of 2001–2003 is to be viewed as something more than a simple *coup d'état* and contest for power unrelieved by genuine intellectual joinder-of-issue, the eventual victors will have to come up with something substantial in the way of new ideas on government and foreign policy. The concept of a "democratic deficit" matching the "financial deficit" successfully overcome by the prime minister and his finance minister by 1998, is an attractive one But it needs to be fleshed out, in terms of concrete and detailed secondary principles for operational application, before it can be taken very seriously or considered as something more than a campaign slogan. In fact, in the indicia so far offered, it seems to fall short of the suggestions already made about two decades ago by the Lefebvre and McGrath Committees on reform of the House of Commons, and to be in no real sense the sort of revolution against old thought-ways and outmoded institutions and processes that the well-informed and well-educated electorate of today is increasingly demanding.

Prime Minister Chrétien, for his part, acting in no sense like a "lame-duck" leader shortly to depart, but rather like someone with the zest for a new mandate — albeit a mandate for posterity — has begun to use the announced interregnum until February 2004, when a new leader will eventually emerge, to chart out an ambitious new agenda, which in a very real sense reflects his own earliest, populist Liberal roots and sentiments. In the demonstrated absence of any real attempt or interest within the parliamentary Liberal caucus to challenge the new Chrétien agenda, or even to engage in a serious and open public debate on it, it may be difficult for any successor as prime minister to reverse the main elements in the Chrétien legacy's politically imaginative and even daring package. One may wonder if the unfolding political events within the Liberal party and caucus might have taken a different course if this new agenda for action had been unveiled earlier — perhaps in 1998, when newly into the second Liberal majority government, or even in December 2000, when a third Liberal majority victory had just been won.

Post-Chrétien Liberalism

Among key policy signposts for what is clearly intended to be the proclaimed new Liberalism for a post-Chrétien era in the party's fortunes are the following:

(1) A realistic acceptance of the limits and also the opportunities of continentalism and the Canada-United States special relationship. There has been a noticeable cooling in the rhetoric of Canada-US relations, which had been unnecessarily exacerbated by off-the-cuff public criticisms by several ministers and some senior civil servants in the post-September 11 period. The prime minister, who has always displayed a studied politeness in his dealings with foreign leaders, clearly had decided to try to develop and maintain an effective personal working relationship with the US president, and to operate through the deputy prime minister in achieving concrete solutions to Canada-US conflicts, and developing common policies. The word has gone out to the rest of the cabinet. This marks an attempt to return to the highly effective "quiet diplomacy" of the Pearson era. The intervention by the prime min-

ister, and the imposition of his own prime-ministerial decisions, seemed politically wise and necessary after apparently conflicting public positions and sometimes self-contradictory statements by ministers charged variously with the defence and foreign policy aspects of the Canada-United States relationship. When he indicated to the House of Commons on 17 March 2003 that Canada would not take part in the US invasion of Iraq, Chrétien took special care to base Canada's decision on the long-standing national commitment to the United Nations and the principle of a necessary prior, explicit legal mandate, through security council resolution, before recourse to the use of force or armed intervention. He deliberately avoided any comment on the legality of the US and British invasion of Iraq, and directed his government colleagues to exercise similar restraint.

(2) A return to the United Nations as the prime arena for Canadian policy-making in foreign affairs. In another vindication of Pearsonian liberalism, the prime minister immediately took up the 8 September 2002 joint initiative of President Chirac and Chancellor Schroeder, in insisting that the prior authority of the UN security council be obtained as a precondition to any armed intervention in the Iraq situation. The concerted action by these three G-8 leaders undoubtedly assisted the US and British governments' decision to proceed through the UN, resulting in a fifteen to zero vote by the UN security council to that effect in Resolution 1441 of 8 November 2002. The US and British subsequent decision to bypass the United Nations and to invade Iraq without any prior, explicit security council resolution authorizing such armed intervention, resulted from their signal failure to be able to assure gaining the necessary minimum of votes in the security council for that purpose. Prime Minister Chrétien, in announcing in the House of Commons on 17 March 2003 that Canada would not take part in the US/British invasion based that decision squarely on the absence of any prior, explicit legal authority from the security council by way of a new resolution.

(3) Acceptance of the "one world" environmental protection imperative. The Prime Minister's successful insistence on a parliamentary vote on the Kyoto Accords (a step legally quite unnecessary and irrelevant to Canada's ratification) will make it politically more difficult for any successor to yield to provincial premiers' objections when the subsequent difficult process of legislative implementation of the Accords in Canada arises concretely. In terms of the Constitution Act of 1867, joint federal and provincial action will be needed, and difficult rounds of intergovernmental negotiations will ensue for the next prime minister.

(4) Setting limits to the power of private banking and financial institutions. The Prime Minister's effective veto on the latest attempts at a merger by two of the five leading commercial banks will strongly reinforce the "grass-roots" opposition within the parliamentary caucus and in the party constituency associations, which had killed the earlier merger attempts during the second Chrétien mandate.

(5) Progress on Indian land treaties within the Constitution Act. The Indian affairs minister, Robert Nault, after an initially shaky start in a traditional "graveyard" ministry for junior ministers, is proceeding with the Prime Minister's blessings on ambitious new plans that will ensure more rapid progress on the remaining land treaties, accompanied by more rigorous application of requirements of constitutional due process and of fiscal responsibility to aboriginal self-government and internal financial management by aboriginal band leaders.

(6) Reform of the Liberal party organization. Reflecting again his earliest populist liberal roots, the prime minister has been moving boldly to remove the appearance of influence by corporate and financial institutions on Liberal party policies by effectively banning corporate (and also trade union) donations to political parties, and by putting a ceiling limit on individual donations as well. Full disclosure of all donations will be required, including monies

given to constituency associations between elections and in party constituency nomination campaigns. There also would be a spending limit for nomination campaigns (something long sought by women candidates). Public funding of political parties would become the norm. If the prime minister and his successors were to link these reforms to new legal controls on the party electoral and nomination processes, they might be in a position to ensure more effective "grass roots" involvement in party management and internal governance, and thus Pierre Trudeau's ideal concept of participatory democracy as constitutional law-in-action in Canada. The federal elections commissioner, apparently responding to the lead provided by the prime minister's announced reforms to party organization, stated that his office, henceforth, would cease transmitting the federal statute-based partial reimbursement of candidates election expenses to party headquarters and would direct the payment instead to candidates' constituency organizations. The federal elections office decision seems constitutionally correct — the party headquarters, as such, having no legal status under the Constitution Act. (There, of course, would be nothing to prevent an already reimbursed election candidate from *voluntarily* sharing part of the payment with the party headquarters.)

Resolving the Contradictions

What may be the defining moment in Jean Chrétien's decade-long prime ministership occurred well into the long constitutional interregnum between the announcement in August 2002 of his intention to step down and the projected date in February 2004 of his actual retirement. It involved establishing contemporary Canadian policies on the use of armed force and armed intervention in the specific-fact context of Iraq and President George W. Bush's ill-concealed, long-range intention to invade Iraq to complete, in the words of some present-day US analysts, what his father, President George H.W. Bush, had supposedly left undone from the Gulf War.

The political-military decision, then, to stop at the Kuwait borders had been made on the advice of the US Chief of the General Staff at the time, General Colin Powell. It reflected both the soldier's professional judgement in favour of economy in the use of power: don't risk going on and unnecessarily killing thousands of innocent civilians if the defined objective of repelling the invaders has already been attained. And don't exceed your previously defined mandate: if you feel it needs expansion, go back to the original granting authority and request it to make the change accordingly. In one of those curious historical ironies, General Powell would go on to head the State Department under the second President Bush and thus to present the US administration's case to the UN security council for the legal licensing of an armed intervention in Iraq in 2003.

Prime Minister Chrétien's task in establishing Canada's policies in response to US pressures to join it in a US-led and directed, renewed collective armed action against Iraq would have to involve striking a necessary balance between Canada's long-standing respect for the primacy of the United Nations to decide on peace or war and the ever-mounting continentalist imperative of coordinating and, if need be at times, subordinating our foreign and defence policies to continental priorities determined in Washington, D.C. When, therefore, Prime Minister Chrétien finally had to make the choice for Canada in March 2003 either to remain faithful to the Lester Pearson/Paul Martin Sr. position from the earlier "golden era" of Canadian foreign policy or to yield instead to the ever stronger importuning of the US neighbour and free trade partner, it was not a decision taken on a *tabula rasa* basis and in an absence of any relevant rules of international law.

Prime Minister Chrétien had been troubled, as evidently had other security council members, permanent and non-permanent, by a lack of clarity in the US administration's arguments in support of an invasion of Iraq. Chrétien, in an address to the US Council on Foreign Relations in Chicago on 13 February 2003, felt it necessary to sound a caution to the US administration against being seen to act unilaterally:

The price of being the world's only superpower is that its motives are sometimes questioned by others. Great strength is not always perceived by others as benign. Not everyone around the world is prepared to take the words of the United States on faith. . . . It is essential that the United States can count on support from around the world. Therefore it is imperative to avoid the perception of a "clash of civilizations." Maximum use of the United Nations will minimize that risk.

In a later extended interview with George Stephanopoulos on the US national television network, ABC, on 9 March 2003, Prime Minister Chrétien was even more specific on the consequences of a US military intervention without the legal authority of a UN umbrella resolution: "Well, it would be quite bad because, you know, the Americans are the only super power now. . . . You have to really be realistic about it, that makes some people nervous. . . . Some do not want to take your [the US] word, you know, too easily; they want to ask questions and they are afraid to have only one super power. That it's dangerous for them." In answer to the specific question as to whether Canada would fight in Iraq *only* if there was a UN resolution, Chrétien replied: "It has been the position of Canada since the first day and it was the position of Canada in 1990 [with the Gulf War]."

Chrétien was also clear and categorical, in the same public interview that UN security council resolution 1441 of 8 November 2002 — the claimed legal basis for a U.S. unilateral armed intervention in Iraq — was concerned with disarmament of the Saddam Hussein regime and nothing more, and certainly not with any forcible change of regime in Iraq: "That [change of regime] is one of the concerns that a lot of people have, you know. China might say, well we have a problem somewhere and you know, we don't like the regime and we're going to change the regime. It's why it's dangerous. You know, everybody will take that as a pretext. . . . Because where do you stop? You know, if its okay that we do that there, why not elsewhere?"

Prime Minister Chrétien made his definitive declaration of Canadian policy on the use of armed force against Iraq, in the House of Commons on 17 March 2003, immediately after the US administration and its main associate, the United Kingdom government, indicated that they would abandon their previously scheduled resolution in the UN security council which would have effectively authorized an armed intervention — this after it had become clear that the US and the UK could not, in spite of all the behind-the-scenes pressures, muster enough votes in the council to reach the minimum total of nine votes necessary for the resolution's adoption, quite apart from the additional hurdle of any French, Russian or Chinese vetoes. Chrétien announced, simply, that if military action were to proceed without a new resolution of the security council, Canada would not participate. He received a sustained standing ovation in the House from the government Liberal MPs to be sure, but also from the opposition *Bloc Québécois* and the NDP Members. In his careful choice of words, he deliberately avoided saying that the planned US invasion of Iraq would violate international law or amount to a war crime.

The conclusion from Canada's role in the political run-up to the US invasion of Iraq on 19 March 2003, without the US and its British cohort having obtained the legal authority of a prior, explicit Security Council Resolution may be resumed as follows:

1) The decision on Canada's position was at all times that of the prime minister acting in this regard in the contemporary full sense of a "presidential" prime minister, and not of the cabinet as a whole or the defence and foreign ministers as the ministers with the most specific sectorial portfolios involved. The sometimes contradictory statements or changes of position coming from these ministers would seem, on the evidence of past practice within the Chrétien administration, to have been tolerated or even encouraged as a means of testing public reactions before the prime minister should announce his own final position.

2) The Prime Minister's final position was not a surprise since it had already been formed and formulated long before the opening of the crucial security council debates in March 2003 that preceded

the US decision unilaterally to invade Iraq. Immediately after the Kosovo operation in 1998–1999, which was made *without* the legal authority of a prior security council resolution, a retrospective legal reexamination commenced in all the main participatory countries in that operation — Britain, France, Germany, the United States and Canada. A key issue had been the legality of military operations conducted outside the United Nations by the anti-Soviet military alliance, NATO, which still survived in the post-Cold War era. The *Institut de Droit International* launched its own inquiry into this basic issue of legality, with key jurists from all the main NATO states serving on its expert commission formed for this purpose. At the conclusion of all these activities, a common *opinio juris* had clearly emerged in favour of maintaining the original, historical position that the United Nations Charter establishes an absolute ban on recourse to armed force or armed intervention without a prior *explicit* enabling resolution from the security council.

3) In announcing Canada's position on the US invasion in the House of Commons on 17 March 2003, Prime Minister Chrétien, as noted earlier, consciously avoided rhetorical flourishes and displayed a prudent economy in his choice of words, limiting himself to stating the Canadian government's policy and deliberately refraining from gratuitous criticism of the US (or British) positions. He, privately, might have wished to have been able to make a speech like that of the French foreign minister, Dominique de Villepin, who maintained the primacy of the United Nations and of international law with a clarity of logical reasoning and an elegance of expression that brought an unprecedented round of public applause in the normally staid and dull security council. That, however, has never been the Chrétien style in advancing a politically difficult position. What is more, in the special context of the new continentalism and Canada-US special relations, it would have been unnecessarily harmful and counterproductive. Chrétien moved in keeping with his long-demonstrated mastery of the political processes and his understanding, ahead of other G-8

leaders, of the force of the new *"People's Power"* in guiding political decisions.[112] He correctly read opinion within his own party in the House of Commons (in spite of recent leadership-succession conflicts), and in the country at large. Within the Liberal party ranks in Ottawa, he didn't lose a single MP, and there were absolutely no public demonstrations against him. Contrast this with the position of the several European leaders who rallied to President Bush! In Britain, one million demonstrators against the British prime minister took to the streets in London, with similarly large public protests in Madrid and in Rome. Within the British House of Commons on 26 February 2003, 122 Labour party MPs joined with seventy-seven MPs from other parties in voting against Prime Minister Blair.[113] On 18 March 2003, immediately after the US-British decision to abandon their attempt to secure a new security council resolution authorizing armed action against Iraq, a number of Labour ministers (including former foreign minister Robin Cook) resigned from cabinet and 139 Labour MPs voted against their prime minister on an anti-war motion.[114]

By comparison, it had been a remarkable *tour de force* for Chrétien. No lame-duck prime minister, but someone determined to

---

[112] Chrétien had profited from the lessons of the APEC (Asia-Pacific Economic Cooperation) summit meeting held in Vancouver in November 1997. The much execrated dictator of Indonesia, Suharto, was greeted, not unexpectedly, by hostile student demonstrations during an APEC leaders' photo opportunity visit to the University of British Columbia at the beginning of a regular working day for the University. In balancing the undoubted public interest in maintaining the dignity and physical well-being of visiting heads-of-state (one of the oldest international law principles, going back to the ancient Persians), and more contemporary public interests in free speech (including public protest and criticism against cruel or corrupt foreign regimes), the federal government — as a belatedly appointed commissioner of enquiry, Ted Hughes, would conclude — applied inappropriate police control conduct. (See Pue, W. Wesley, ed., *Pepper in Our Eyes: The APEC Affair,* Vancouver: UBC Press, 2000.)

[113] The final vote was 399-199 in favour of Blair (with the opposition Conservatives supporting the government).

[114] The final vote (with opposition Conservative support) was 396 to 217 in favour of the government, but Blair had lost one-third of his own party.

impose his own continuing presence during the long interregnum until his pre-announced retirement in February 2004. His skills in carrying his cabinet, his MPs and his party with him in the enunciation of a new Chrétien Doctrine — supplementing the original Pearson emphasis on the UN as the prime arena for our policy-making in foreign affairs — on not engaging Canada or Canadians in the use of armed force or armed interventions except with the prior, explicit authority of the United Nations security council or in exercise of the right to self-defence as strictly defined and limited under the UN Charter, may well be his most important legacy. Judging from the warmth with which it has been greeted, not merely by the traditional "founding" Canadian communities — French and English — but also by the new cultural communities, the Chrétien Doctrine corresponds very well with the new pluralism of today's inclusive, multi-cultural Canadian society. It is unlikely that any future federal Liberal party leader would wish to depart from that.

The expectation today is that the friendly neighbour relationship with the United States must be a robust one and not one of servility or mute acquiescence. The respect and mutual give-and-take inherent in such a relationship ensures, reciprocally, that Canadian efforts — with the strong support of US Senators and Congressmen and Governors of border states — to achieve and maintain open frontiers and free movement of goods and services and people across the common international boundary, are maintained and extended. And this with full respect, on the Canadian side, for the special concerns on the US side, in the post-September 11, 2001 era, for US security and public safety.

BOOKS BY EDWARD MCWHINNEY,
Q.C., LL.M., S.J.D., LL.D.

———

AUTHORED:

1. *Judicial Review in the English-Speaking World* (first edition 1956, fourth edition 1969);

2. *Föderalismus und Bundesverfassungsrecht* (1962);

3. *Comparative Federalism: States' Rights and National Power* (first edition 1962, second edition 1965);

4. *Constitutionalism in Germany and the Federal Constitutional Court* (1962);

5. *Peaceful Coexistence and Soviet-Western International Law* (1964);

6. *Federal Constitution-Making for a Multi-National World* (1966);

7. *International Law and World Revolution* (1967);

8. *Conflit idéologique et Ordre public mondial* (1970);

9. *Parliamentary Privilege and the Publication of Parliamentary Debates* (1974);

10. *The Illegal Diversion of Aircraft and International Law* — the 1973 Hague Academy lectures (1975);

11. *The International Law of Détente: Arms Control, European Security, and East-West Co-operation* (1978);

12. *The World Court and the Contemporary International Law-Making Process* (1979);

13. *Quebec and the Constitution, 1960–1978* (1979);

14. *Conflict and Compromise: International Law and World Order in a Revolutionary Age* (1981);

15. *Constitution-Making: Principles, Process, Practice* (1981);

16. *Canada and the Constitution, 1979–1982: Patriation and the Charter of Rights* (1982);

17. *United Nations Law-Making (1984) / Les Nations Unies et la Formation du Droit* (1986);

18. *Supreme Courts and Judicial Law Making: Constitutional Tribunals and Constitutional Review* (1986);

19. *Aerial Piracy and International Terrorism* (1987);

20. *The International Court of Justice and Western Tradition of International Law* — 1986 Paul Martin Lectures, University of Windsor (1987);

21. *Nuclear Weapons and Contemporary International Law* (1988);

22. *Judicial Settlement of International Disputes: Jurisdiction, Justiciability and Judicial Law-Making on the Contemporary International Court of Justice* — 1990 Hague Academy lectures (1991);

23. *Judge Shigeru Oda and the Progressive Development of International Law: Opinions on the International Court of Justice, 1976–1992* (1993);

24. *Judge Manfred Lachs and Judicial Law-Making: Opinions on the International Court of Justice, 1967–1993* (1995);

25. *The United Nations and a New World Order for a New Millennium: Self-Determination, State Succession, and Humanitarian Intervention* (2000);

26. *Self-Determination of Peoples and Plural-Ethnic States: Secession and State Succession, and the Alternative Federal Option* — 2002 Hague Academy Lectures (2003).

CO-AUTHORED OR EDITED:

27. *Canadian Jurisprudence: The Civil Law and Common Law in Canada* (1958);

28. *Law, Foreign Policy, and the East-West Détente* (1964);

29. *Esquema de un Curso Basico de Derecho International Publico* (with F. Cuevas Cancino, 1964);

30. *The Freedom of the Air* (with M.A. Bradley, 1968);

31. *New Frontiers in Space Law* (with M.A. Bradley, 1969);

32. *The International Law of Communications* (1970);

33. *Aerial Piracy and International Law* (1971);

34. *Federalism and Supreme Courts and the Integration of Legal Systems* (with Pierre Pescatore, 1973);

35. *La situation de la langue française au Québec, en trois tomes* (*avec* J.D. Gendron, et al, l973);

36. *Municipal Government in a New Canadian Federal System* (1980);

37. *Mécanismes pour une nouvelle Constitution* (with Edmond Orban, et al, 1981);

38. *From Co-Existence to Cooperation: International Law and Organization in the Post- Cold War Era* (with G.I. Tunkin and V.S. Vereshchetin, 1991);

39. *Federalism-in-the-Making: Contemporary Canadian and German Constitutionalism, National and Transnational* (with J. Zaslove and W. Wolf, 1992);

40. *Liber Amicorum Judge Shigeru Oda, volumes one and two* (with Nisuke Ando and Rüdiger Wolfrum, 2002).

In addition, Dr. McWhinney has contributed chapters to 151 other books on constitutional, legal, and international affairs, published nearly two hundred articles in learned journals and the popular press, and written over 300 published book reviews. For a complete list of his publications, see *McWhinney Bibliography* compiled and confirmed by the reference section of the Library of Parliament, Ottawa, 1995 and 2000 (Ian McDonald, editor).

ABOUT THE AUTHOR

Ted McWhinney gained his commission in the Air Force at the age of nineteen in the closing years of World War II. After completing professional and advanced degrees at Yale University, he undertook post-doctoral researches in The Hague, Berlin, Pisa, and Geneva. After appointments as Lecturer and Assistant Professor on the faculties of the Yale Law School and Yale College and Graduate School, he went on to full professorial chairs at the University of Toronto, McGill, Indiana, and Simon Fraser in Vancouver. He has taught as a Visiting Professor in Universities around the World — among others, at the University of Paris I (Sorbonne) (in 1968, 1982 and 1985); the Collège de France in Paris; Heidelberg and the Max Planck-Institut (in 1960–1 and 1990); The Hague Academy of International Law (in 1973, 1990 and 2002); the University of Madrid; the Institut-Universitaire of Luxembourg; the Aristotle University, Thessaloniki; the Meiji University in Tokyo; the Chinese Institute of Contemporary International Relations in Beijing; and within Canada at the Université Laval in Quebec. In addition, he has lectured extensively at universities and academies in Eastern Europe and the former Soviet Union, and in India. His published books and other writings have been translated into nine languages. He has been a consultant to the UN Secretary General, member and special adviser to the Canadian delegation to the UN General Assembly for three years in the early 1980s, and Member of the Permanent Court of Arbitration in The Hague. He is a Member and Past President (1999–2001) of the *Institut de Droit International* (Geneva); and Member of the *Académie Internationale de Droit Comparé* (Paris). In public life in Canada, he was Member of Parliament for Vancouver Quadra for two successive terms, and Parliamentary Secretary (Fisheries and Oceans) and Parliamentary Secretary (Foreign Affairs). He chose not to run for re-election for a third Parliamentary term, and returned to his earlier engagement in national and international affairs as a writer and lecturer and adviser.

INDEX

AGMV Marquis

MEMBRE DE SCABRINI MEDIA

Quebec, Canada
2003